Investigate & Connect

Earth & Space
SCIENCE

by David A. Wiley
& Christine A. Royce

Cover illustration by
Matthew Van Zomeren

Inside illustrations by
Marc F. Johnson

Publisher
Instructional Fair • TS Denison
Grand Rapids, Michigan 49544

Instructional Fair • TS Denison

About the Authors

David A. Wiley, Ed.D. is Chair and Associate Professor at the University of Scranton in Pennsylvania. He has over twenty-five years in education and is a frequent presenter of classroom teaching strategies to elementary and middle school teachers. Many of his publications and presentations center on the theme of teaching across the curriculum using science and children's literature. A triple hitter, Dr. Wiley holds his Bachelors, Masters, and Doctorate from the Science Education Program at Temple University. His main research interests include the integration of science instruction across the school curriculum by using the S-T-S theme, and the use of children's literature to enhance the teaching of science in the elementary and middle grades.

Christine A. Royce is currently the Academic Dean at Bishop Hannan High School in Scranton, Pennsylvania. She has nine years teaching experience at the elementary through high school level. Presently a doctoral student in Science Education at Temple University, she holds her Bachelors in Elementary Education and Masters in Curriculum/Instruction and Administration and Supervision. She sits on the CBC-NSTA Outstanding Science Trade Book Review Panel and serves as a manuscript reviewer for *Science and Children* (NSTA publication). She was named the 1997 Presidential Awardee for Excellence in Mathematics and Science Teaching for Pennsylvania.

Credits

Authors: David A. Wiley & Christine A. Royce
Cover Illustration: Matthew Van Zomeren
Inside Illustrations: Marc F. Johnson
Project Director: Debra Olson Pressnall
Editors: Debra Olson Pressnall & Karen Seberg
Cover Art Production: Matthew Van Zomeren
Graphic Layout: Deborah Hanson McNiff

Standard Book Number: 1-56822-478-8
Earth & Space Science
Copyright © 1999 by Ideal • Instructional Fair Publishing Group
2400 Turner Avenue NW
Grand Rapids, Michigan 49544

Table of Contents

How to Use This Book

As classroom teachers we are well aware of the *myriad tasks* that face you on a daily basis in your professional life. Time is your worst enemy. Research, planning, and preparation are all activities which must precede instruction. This book was written in an attempt to assist you in preparing, in a time-efficient way, for quality science instruction. The structure of this book was designed with you in mind. The book is divided into a number of sections. The first section deals with how the book can be used in an inquiry-based environment. Information is also provided on how trade books can be selected for your classroom as well as a number of web sites that you and your students can use to find additional information.

Subsequent sections of the book are referred to as modules and provide you with the in-depth information, activities, and connections to help you in your classroom. Features of every module include:

- **Science background:** Provides a brief explanation of the science concepts needed for a basic understanding of the science discipline being discussed. A number of diagrams are included to assist in clarification of the ideas presented. More importantly, references to the activities are also provided in context within the section.

- **Annotated bibliography:** This comprehensive list of books includes a brief summary of each title. This bibliography was written to assist you in locating children's literature that can be used with each activity.

- **Activities:** Each activity is presented in a lesson plan format that provides you with information relating to the objectives that the activity addresses, a list of materials needed for the activity, and the procedure to follow in conducting the activity. A section on related children's literature specific to the activity is given and the books listed are described in the annotated bibliography. The final section of each activity consists of connections to other subject areas that may be explored. Inquiry-based student lab pages are provided for most of the activities to assist you in the lessons.

As you use this book it is important to realize that activities can be adapted to meet the needs of your students and your classroom environment. There is no set formula for accomplishing this task. The expert on your students' capabilities and behavior is you. We cannot make absolute suggestions as to how you will adapt any-thing in this book to your particular situation with your particular students. Each of the activities can be adapted for students who are very talented simply by letting them do more of the exploring. You may wish to ask more questions at the end of each investigation, or have students use journals to record predictions, prior knowledge, and then what they learned from the investigation. You may ask them how their results can be applied in the real world around them. These strategies are effective in making the activities more challenging for the students.

Each of the activities can be adapted for students who are not skilled in science investigation simply by giving more direction. Depending on the activity, you may prefer to lead the students through the activity by example, step by step, with the entire class in unison. For some students it may be best to read and review the instructions as a group before beginning the investigation. Perhaps the best procedure for some activities is to have the students complete one task each day over a period of several days. Some of the activities within this book may not be appropriate for your students to complete. In that case, you may want the students to simply watch, and/or take notes, and/or answer questions regarding activities you choose to do as demonstrations.

For the activities that you choose to do as student-centered, hands-on and minds-on science experiences, you have many choices for organizing your class. You may consider grouping the students in your classroom; in most activities, groups of two to five can be effective. While large groups require fewer materials and equipment as a class unit, they are sometimes difficult to manage. Large groups may also cut down on the active participation of each student. Groups of three are favored by the authors, although the research on ideal group size is not definitive. The key is to structure the activities in a way that works for you as the manager of a classroom environment.

The materials, including equipment and supplies, required for each activity are appropriate for a small group or individual. Many of the listed items are inexpensive or easy to locate; while some science equipment must be purchased if not available in your school. For sources of the equipment, you may wish to consider commercial suppliers if you have a budget for purchasing materials. If you only have a small budget for science, you may consider contacting your senior high school science department as a source of materials and equipment, such a balances. In most science departments, supplies of the kind required in this book are not rare. For example, hydrochloric acid is usually stored in concentrated forms in gallon jugs, and making a dilute solution for you does not represent a problem for the science specialist. In fact, being used as a resource by an elementary/middle school teacher would be a compliment for most high school science teachers.

Inquiry-Based Instruction

Individual Differences

Most teachers realize after their initial contact with teaching that not all students and not all classes are going to be able to learn at the same levels as other students or other classes. This is especially true with teaching science to elementary/middle school students. In the elementary school classroom, great differences in both ability and background experiences exist between classes and even among individual students in each class. Taking these conditions into account is an important aspect of planning for effective instruction in science. The differences can range from the specific kinds of experiences each student has while very young to the social structure in which the student is raised. The degree of familiarity with the natural environment, for example, may be different in the eyes of an urban student than the view of a Native American. Some students may be familiar with the sensations like "losing your stomach" while flying in air-planes, while others may only have a passing familiarity with the same sensation as experienced on a Ferris wheel ride. Accounting for these differences makes this aspect of planning especially important with the approach favored by the authors, the inquiry approach. An examination of the students, their abilities and their backgrounds, can save a great amount of time and frustration on the part of both student and instructor.

What Is Inquiry?

The inquiry approach to science teaching involves more than simply asking students questions about science content. Inquiry includes three components as follows: Students must identify questions and problems that precede answers in the learning process, process information mentally to achieve meaningful under-standing, and students must be actively involved in the learning (Cairn, 1993). The term *inquiry*, as used in this book, reflects the three components of inquiry as identified above, and the activities within this book utilize all three compo-nents. The objectives for activities represent the questions (problems, topics, or issues) to be studied. The instructional sequences given within the activities is presented with the assumption that students can perform the activities and be, thus, active learners. Further, questions are offered to guide the students toward an understanding of the science that will be both meaningful and persistent.

Levels of Inquiry

What makes a lesson an inquiry lesson, and is all inquiry the same? To answer this question, it is important to understand that there are three segments in any lesson involving an investigation. In the first segment, a problem (or topic or issue) must be identified for investigation. In the second, an appropriate methodology must be established for the accomplishment of the objectives of the lesson. Finally in the third, the conclusions must be drawn as a result of the investigation. The process of inquiry can be adjusted to meet the needs of any group of students by providing more or less information in each of these segments, and by expecting the students to answer correspondingly less or more. At least three levels of inquiry exist and make this form of teaching very different from expository teaching. The various levels of inquiry, from expository (none to very little inquiry) to full inquiry (with the teacher giving little or no information) are summarized below:

EXPOSITORY TEACHING

In expository teaching, the teacher establishes all aspects of the inquiry lesson by establishing what problem will be taught, how the problem will be approached, and the teacher will even draw conclusions for the class. This method is, in some circles, known as the "talking head" and is, unfortunately, a dominant form of instruction in science education. "The present science textbooks and methods of instruction, far from helping, often actually impede progress toward scientific literacy. They emphasize the learning of answers more than the exploration of questions, memory at the expense of critical thought, bits and pieces of information instead of understandings in context, recitation over argument, reading in lieu of doing" (American Association for the Advancement of Science, 1990, p. xvi). Too often, a book becomes the single focus of all learning in science. One study states that "90 percent of all science teachers use a textbook 95 percent of the time" (Bonnstetter, Penick, & Yager, 1983, p. 3). Thus the text becomes the single source of information and the single source of activity for over 95 percent of the time. While expository teaching is an efficient technique to communicate large amounts of information, it is certainly not inquiry.

PRIMARY LEVEL OF INQUIRY

An initial experience with inquiry can be found in the experience of virtually all teachers. At the primary level of inquiry teaching, the teacher establishes the problem and the methodology, but allows the students to draw their own conclusions. This is the format for the majority of lab investigations to which many teachers are exposed in their own education. Usually given by a lab handout, the objectives (problem) of the investigation are established. The handout also provides the methodology through a carefully sequenced series of steps, and then leads the students with questions to draw their own conclusions. Since the teacher usually has already directly taught the concepts involved in the lab exercise, this requires very little inquiry since the student already knows the answer. Only when students are given the freedom to draw their own conclusions does inquiry begin. When the students ask themselves "What does this mean?" they will, perhaps, begin to build their own frameworks for understanding within the common experience of the structured investigation.

SECONDARY LEVEL OF INQUIRY

The secondary level of inquiry represents a higher level of inquiry in that the students are asked to establish their own methodologies to yield their own conclusions to a problem that is posed by the teacher. In the elementary classroom, and even at higher levels, the selection of methodology is most often monitored through a requirement of a "proposal" of some sort. In this way, the teacher can actively guide the student toward a methodology that will not lead the student down a path that goes nowhere. The teacher can consider the capabilities of the students and the limitations of equipment available to the students. If the teacher permits the students to pursue an investigation for a long period of time and the students do not see success, then the students can be easily frustrated. The teacher becomes less of a fount of knowledge and more of a guide for student experiences. It is this involvement of the teacher that gives the primary and secondary levels of inquiry the name "guided inquiry."

FULL INQUIRY

In the elementary school, it is very rare to see open inquiry. In open or third level inquiry, the students select the topic to be studied, the methods to be used, and then draw their own conclusions that result from the investigation. This type of inquiry can be independent investigations, such as those in "junior academy of science" projects and in some "gifted student" programs, but is rarely used in the mainstream of elementary education. The reason is, simply, that most of the students at the elementary level are not ready or do not possess the cognitive development to deal effectively with all three aspects demanded by open inquiry. Due to their lack of experiences, it is unreasonable to expect that most elementary students are able to select a problem for investigation that is appropriate to a science concept being studied. Guided inquiry, the preferred methodology at the elementary level, avoids the complexities involved in open inquiry while providing a shared experience in which the learning of science can be enjoyed with a minimum of frustration.

Planning the Investigations

The lessons included within this book are written at the level of primary inquiry. That is, they have expressed objectives, and a carefully sequenced series of steps that permit a successful guided-inquiry investigation. However, the science lessons suggested here can be altered to be suitable for any group of students by adapting the lessons appropriately. To make the investigation less an inquiry and more an expository type of approach, give the students more information regarding the results. Perhaps inclusion of a "You should see . . . which is . . . " statement would accomplish just that. If you wish to increase the amount of inquiry involved in the lessons, then avoid giving step-by-step directions and allow the students to construct their own procedures. (See reproducible form on page 8.) Again, the use of the "proposal" is encouraged for this type of investigation. Use your professional judgment to decide whether to increase or decrease the level of inquiry expected of groups of students.

Planning Your Investigation

Questions: _____
(Purpose) _____

Materials _____
Needed: _____
_____
_____

Procedure: Design an experiment.

Steps in Your Procedure

1.

2.

3.

4.

5.

Results: Record observations and/or collect data. (Examples: Keep a log. Draw diagrams. Make a chart or table.)

Conclusion: _____
_____
_____

Choosing and Using Trade Books

National Use of This Methodology

The use of children's literature in the teaching of science has become an increasingly popular methodology that has garnered much national attention. Many elementary teachers are using literature in their science programs as part of a literacy-based instruction because it blends reading, writing, and talking in a learning environment. Teachers realize that there are many possibilities for developing activities from these books that allow students to explore science in a hands-on/minds-on environment. Further, we know that science-oriented trade books are very popular with children. Children's trade books can serve as a valuable reading resource. A year-long study done by a librarian in New York shows that science books are the second most popular books among children (Mechling & Oliver, 1983, p. 37). For purposes of this methodology, trade books or children's literature can be defined as any "commercially available publication that can be used as a supplement to your classroom text" (Kralina, 1993, p. 33). This may include fiction as well as nonfiction books.

However popular this practice is, this methodology is not without naysayers. While some research supports the use of children's literature, other studies suggest that there can be problems with using children's literature in the teaching and learning of science. It is questionable which side has more supporting evidence. It is quite obvious in the world of practice that many teachers put a great deal of time into the integration of trade books into an activity-based science curriculum. However, in a literature search on the topic, very little quantitative support for the use of trade books to teach science was found. One quasi-experimental study showed that by combining the instructional time allotted for reading and science, students' achievement in science was at significantly higher levels (Romance & Vitale, 1992). However, another study suggests that "children's literature may not be an effective science resource" due to its ability to foster misconceptions (Mayer, 1995). It is clear that this methodology is being utilized by elementary teachers throughout our schools since many of the articles in journals are based on classroom experiences—a kind of research in action rather than quantitative research. Qualitative research confirms the value of the following suggestions: Given the degree to which this methodology is embraced, it is important for classroom teachers to understand both the benefits and pitfalls of using children's literature for science instruction.

Benefits to Reading

One of the primary benefits in using trade books is the possibility of addressing interest areas and reading levels of students. Researchers (Tunnell & Jacobs, 1989; Holmes & Ammon, 1985; Simon, 1982) have shown that the use of trade books increases the students' interest levels, improves reading skills, and allows for individuality and variability for students with different reading abilities. This methodology has also shown to be an important tool in aiding students to develop an appreciation of reading for pleasure (Simon, 1982). When children read for pleasure, science trade books offer the opportunity of teaching the students when students do not realize that they are learning. (Simon, 1982).

Not only does the use of trade books address the varying reading levels of students, there is also the possibility to increase reading abilities. Research [Cohen, 1968; Cullinan, Jaggar & Strickland, 1974; Eldredge & Butterfield, 1986 (cited in Tunnell & Jacobs, 1989)] goes on to show that the use of children's literature in the reading program had a statistically significant outcome in terms of increased reading levels compared to the traditional approaches to reading instruction. Gee & Olson (1992) also point out that the use of trade books in a primary science curriculum strengthens students' basic skills and helps them read more difficult books.

Children in the elementary grades are taught how to read using stories. When they attempt to read science textbooks they find that reading this material is very different from what they are accustomed to in reading class. Textbooks offer a heavy concentration of factual information that is expressed in an expository format rather than the narrative format found in reading. Therefore, by using children's literature, students are being presented factual and conceptual information in the manner that parallels their reading instruction, allowing for both science and reading to be strengthened.

Benefits to Science

When children's literature is carefully chosen, many benefits can occur. These benefits include addressing the individual needs of learners through a variety of materials; allowing them to explore science and the scientific method in a different perspective; providing students with knowledge from a wholistic perspective about their natural world; encouraging them to develop critical thinking abilities through reading; and enlarging their vocabularies (Janke & Norton, 1983).

One of the benefits that exists is the availability of science trade books for use within the elementary/middle school classroom. In recent years, an abundance of elementary trade books that teach science have made it possible to teach nearly every science unit with this methodology (Crook & Lehman, 1990). By having a greater selection of trade books from which to choose, teachers can easily meet the individual needs of children by providing several selections on the same topic rather than attempting to use one textbook.

When a familiar format is used instead of a textbook, each student is not as overwhelmed with the facts and has an opportunity to view science from a different perspective. Through the use of children's literature, students are able to see science as an integral part of their daily lives (Stiffler, 1992). Children are also able to make connections to real life applications when facts are presented versus when they are taught only through traditional means. Once students see science as a part of their lives, attitudes toward science improve as does their attitudes toward scientists.

The use of trade books also allows the teacher to use children's interests to guide the teaching of science (Simon, 1982). Crook & Lehman argue that "if they are engaged in the content of the book, drawn to its detailed illustrations, photographs, paintings, woodcuts, diagrams, children read and learn with enthusiasm" (1990, p. 22).

The question of science achievement within this methodology has been addressed in studies by Romance & Vitale (1992); Dole & Johnson, (1981); Anderson, (1993). These studies show that the incorporation of children's literature into a science program increased the students' science knowledge level, as positive attitudes toward science. Norris' (1989) study showed no significant results but did state that "although enthusiasm for literature was not measured . . . students enjoyed listening to the variety of stories. They would come in each day eager to hear another story. Their enthusiasm for books was very obvious." Additional, non-quantitative studies by Butzow & Butzow (1988); Butzow & Butzow (1990), and Pond & Hoch (1992) show that there is a strong but undefined interrelationship between reading and science when children's literature is used. Research has shown that students may be able to better understand science information when it is presented in a trade book. The trade book contains a story line which is easier to follow than attempting to comprehend facts presented in a science textbook.

The use of trade books in science also aids in the explanation of abstract science principles that are often presented in a confusing way in textbooks. The story line in a trade book is easier for students to follow than the facts that are presented in a textbook (Butzow & Butzow, 1989). The means to help students overcome misconceptions also exists when trade books are used to convey information (Miller, 1996). By using children's trade books to explain abstract concepts and counter misconceptions, students are also developing critical thinking skills (Kralina, 1993). Due to this reading modification, it is argued that using trade books can introduce the student to the scientific method, transmit knowledge about the world, and permit an opportunity to experience the excitement of discovery (Janke & Norton, 1983). Additionally, there is a natural connection between science and reading. It has been shown that many of the skills developed for problem-solving in science are the same skills used by children in reading (Carter & Simpson, 1978). Thus, the research supports the practice of teaching science through children's literature.

Suggestions for Choosing Children's Literature

Although children's literature provides many benefits, one must be careful to select literature of high quality. The following guidelines offer points to consider when selecting and using literature.

APPROPRIATE THEME CONTENT

The first suggestion for selecting literature is to choose trade books that are clearly related to a subject matter theme (Pond & Hoch, 1992; Mayer, 1995; Janke & Norton, 1983). Many forms of assistance to the classroom teacher are available, including the annual list of the National Science Teachers Association—Children's Book Council "Outstanding Trade Books in Science" list which is published in March of each year. There are also a number of articles in journals that present collections of trade books organized into appropriate themes. Such articles typically list appropriate resources for a single or multiple themes and are often followed by a listing of the cited trade books organized by grade level.

GRAPHIC ORGANIZERS

A second suggestion is to use graphic organizers to clarify the science content of the trade books. With many science concepts comes a measure of mystery. Utilizing graphic organizers adds the important aspect of visualization and often makes the concept more concrete and less mysterious in the minds of children (Schwab & Coble, 1985).

OPPORTUNITY TO INVESTIGATE

The third suggestion is to include with the scientific information, opportunities for students to experiment with the concepts. Barrow, Kristo, & Andrew (1984) explain that hands-on/minds-on activities are needed since "according to Piaget's theory, teaching that uses only reading or telling for science is inappropriate for children at the preoperational and concrete operational stages" (p. 188).

Cautions for Use

As noted earlier, not all the literature on the use of trade books is supportive of this methodology. Some of the recent literature has introduced a note of caution in the enormously popular move to teach science using trade books. One of the reasons for such caution is that the accuracy of scientific content sometimes suffers in a trade book's attempt to represent otherwise complicated information. Misinformation is not the only form of inaccuracy that makes its way into children's trade books. Errors of omission or an attempt to simplify the information presented may also be misleading to students.

Some additional warnings regarding the use of science trade books include insuring that stereotypes are avoided, that illustrations are accurate and labeled, that texts encourage scientific ways of thinking, and that science content is clarified by the organization of the book (Janke & Norton, 1983).

Checklist for Selecting Literature

The following checklist can be used in evaluating children's trade books for use in teaching science.

Content

Does the book have:
• an appropriate reading level?
• the interest range for your students?
• an appropriate amount of detail?

Does the book address:
• the subject matter?
• the intended concepts and facts to support them?

Does the book:
• avoid stereotypes?
• encourage analytical thinking?

Can the book:
• be connected to the curriculum's scope and sequence?
• be connected to the textbook?
• be connected to other subject areas?

Illustrations, Pictures, and Diagrams

Do the illustrations, pictures, and diagrams:
• show accurate material?
• have labels that explain them?
• reflect the material that is presented in the text?
• complement the book's text?

Accuracy and Authenticity

Does the book:
• present information in an accurate way?
• present misconceptions or partial truths?
• contain current science information?

Portals for Learning: Web Sites

EARTH SCIENCE

http://ceps.nasm.edu/NASMDOCS/LINKS/ASLINKS.html
     A list of vast resources on the earth sciences

http://www.usgs.gov/
     USGS homepage which includes an index of on-line resources for earth science

GEOLOGY

http://btpdx1.phy.uni-bayreuth.de/solar/tervolc.htm#movie
     High quality images and movies regarding volcanoes

http://sfbay.yahoo.com/external/usgs
     Lists and locations of earthquakes in the San Francisco Bay region

http://volcano.und.nodak.edu/
     Volcano world home page with guides to lots of links

http://www.dfd.dlr.de/app/land/volcano/iceland/Press.html.en
     A story of the volcano eruption in southern Iceland
     If not available, use: www/dfd.dlr.de
     Search for "volcano and Iceland."

http://gldss7.cr.usgs.gov
     The National Earthquake Information Center collects and analyzes information on earthquakes.
     Use the web site to find the location and size of worldwide earthquakes.

http://www.nps.gov/navo/
     Hawaii Volcanoes National Park homepage

http://www.geosociety.org/
     The Geological Society of America homepage

http://www.agu.org/
     The American Geophysical Union homepage

http://www.agiweb.org/
     The American Geological Institute homepage

http://www.aapg.org/
     The American Association of Petroleum Geologists homepage

http://volcano1.pgd.hawaii.edu/goes/index.shtml/
     The GOES 8/10 Hotspot Images web site is hosted by Hawai'i Institute of Geophysics and
     Planetology. The web site displays images that are transmitted from NOAA GOES 8 and 10
     satellites.

METEOROLOGY

http://www.weather.com/twc/homepage.twc
> The Weather Channel site for weather across the nation

http://iwin.nws.noaa.gov/iwin/main.html
> Homepage for the National Weather Service Interactive Weather Information Network

http://www.nssl.noaa.gov/~spc/
> Homepage of the Storm Prediction Center of the University of Oklahoma at Norman

http://www.wmo.ch/web/gcos/gcoshome.html
> Homepage of the Global Climate Observing System with information and data

http://marrella.meteor.wisc.edu/occlusion.html
> Homepage of the University of Wisconsin Occlusion Research homepage which details the development of occluded front.

http://rossby.larc.nasa.gov/
> Description of Three-dimensional Modeling Studies of Atmospheric Chemistry and Transport Processes

http://hydromodel.com/example.htm
> Object Watershed Link Simulation (OWLS) homepage giving examples of graphical output from OWLS

http://www.tessa.org
> Homepage of the Texas Severe Storms Association with good data and links

http://www.miamisci.org/hurricane/
> The Miami Museum of Science homepage featuring the study of hurricanes

OCEANOGRAPHY

http://www.athena.ivv.nasa.gov/curric/oceans/drifters/ocecur.html
> Web page related to the study of ocean currents through the use of drifting buoys

http://www.athena.ivv.nasa.gov/index.html
> Web page for the index to curriculum materials related to oceanography

http://www.nos.noaa.gov/nos/links.html
> Web page for connecting to National Oceanic and Atmospheric Administration sites

gopher://esdim1.esdim.noaa.gov:70/11/noaa_systems/education
> Textual references that give answers to commonly asked questions about the ocean

http://www.ocean98.org/frames.html
> Homepage of the United Nations Year of the Ocean, Ocean98

http://sio.ucsd.edu/
> Homepage of the Scripps Institute for Oceanographic Research

http://www.mbari.org/
　　　Homepage of the Monteray Bay Aquarium Research Institute

http://www-ocean.tamu.edu/~baum/oceanography.html
　　　Homepage listing lessons and activities on oceanography

http://seawifs.gsfc.nasa.gov/ocean_planet.html
　　　Homepage of the Smithsonian's traveling ocean-planet exhibit

ASTRONOMY

http://www.athena.ivv.nasa.gov/curric/space/planets/topics.html
　　　Web site for curriculum materials regarding the planets

http://shuttle.nasa.gov
　　　Homepage for information regarding the shuttle systems

http://tommy.jsc.nasa.gov/~woodfill/SPACEED/SEHHTML/seh.html
　　　Homepage on space education resources

http://www.hq.nasa.gov/education
　　　Homepage of the National Aeronautics and Space Administration

http://www.spacelink.nasa.gov
　　　Online service offers teacher's guides along with images and computer software.

http://www.spacelink.msfc.nasa.gov/CORE
　　　Use this web site to obtain educational materials from the National Aeronautics and Space
　　　Administration.

http://www.quest/arc.nasa.gov
　　　Can communicate with NASA scientists at this web site.

http://www.challenger.org
　　　Homepage of the challenger centers

http://www.cea.berkeley.edu/Education/Ed_resourcelist.html
　　　Lessons and activities related to space science

http://oposite.stsci.edu/pubinfo/edugroup/educational-activities.html
　　　Information on the Space Telescope Science Institute

http://www.exploratorium.edu/learning_studio/cool/space_science.html
　　　The Exploratorium homepage listing "cool" sites to visit related to space science

http://www.eecs.umich.edu/mathscience/funexperiments/agesubject/astronomy.html
　　　Answers to questions related to astronomy that also provides interactive demonstrations

http://spaceboy.nasda.go.jp/Note/Rocket/E/Roc01_e.html
　　　This web site offers facts about rockets—how they fly and more.

References

Anderson, L. S. (1993). "The Effect of Literature-based and Written Composition-based Instructional Strategies on Children's Understanding of Herpetology" (Doctoral dissertation, University of South Carolina, 1993). *Dissertation Abstracts International*, 54: 1230A.

Barrow, L. H., & Salesi, R. A. (1982). "Integrating Science Activities through Literature Webs," *School Science and Mathematics* 82: 65-70.

Barrow, L. H., & Kristo, J. V., & Andrew, B. (1984). "Building Bridges between Science and Reading," *The Reading Teacher* 38 (2): 188-192.

Bonnstetter, R. J., Penick, J. E., & Yager, R. E. (1983). *Teachers in Exemplary Programs: How Do They Compare?* Washington, D.C.: National Science Teachers Association.

Butzow, C. M., & Butzow, J.W. (1988). *Science, Technology, and Society as Experienced through Children's Literature.* (ERIC Document Reproduction Service No. ED 294 141).

_____ (1989). *Science through Children's Literature: An Integrated Approach.* Englewood, CO: Teacher Ideas Press.

_____ (1990). "Science through Children's Literature: An Integrated Approach," *Science Activities* 27 (3): 29-38.

Caduto, M. J., & Bruhac, J. (1994). "There's Science in That Story!" *Instructor* 103 (7): 42-44, 48, 92.

Cairn, A. A. (1993). *Teaching Science through Discovery* (7th ed). Columbus, OH: Merrill.

Carter, & Simpson (1978). "Science and Reading: A Basic Duo," Science Teacher 45 (3): 20.

Crook, P. R., & Lehman, B. A. (1990). "On Track with Trade Books," *Science and Children:* 22-23.

Dole, J. A., & Johnson, V. R. (1981). "Beyond the Textbook: Science Literature for Young People," *Journal of Reading* 24: 579-581.

Galda, L., & MacGregor, P. (1992). "Nature's Wonders: Books for a Science Curriculum," *The Reading Teacher* 46: 236-245.

Gee, T. C., & Olson, M. W. (1992). "Let's Talk Trade Books," *Science and Children* 29 (6): 13-15.

Holmes, B. C., & Ammon, R. I. (1985). "Teaching Content with Trade Books: A Strategy," *Childhood Education* 61: 366-370.

Janke, D., & Norton, D. (1983). "Science Trades in the Classroom: Good Tools for Teachers," *Science and Children* 20 (6): 46-48.

Kralina, L. (1993). "Tricks of the Trade," *The Science Teacher* 60 (9): 33-37.

Mayer, D. A. (1995). "How Can We Best Use Children's Literature in Teaching Science Concepts?" *Science and Children* 32 (6): 16-19, 43-44.

McDonald, J., & Czerniak, C. (1994). "Developing Interdisciplinary Units: Strategies and Examples," *School Science and Mathematics* 94 (1): 5-10.

Mechling, K. R., & Oliver, D. L. (1983). *Science Teachers' Basic Skills.* Volume 1. Washington, D.C.: National Science Teachers Association.

Miller, K. W., Steiner, S. F., & Larson, C.D. (1996). "Strategies for Science Learning," *Science and Children* 33 (6): 24-27, 61.

Norris, L. K. (1989). "The Effects of Integrating Children's Literature into the Kindergarten Science Curriculum. (ERIC Document Reproduction No. ED 314 712).

Orlich, D. C. (1989). "Science Inquiry in the Commonplace," *Science and Children* 26 (6): 22-24.

Pond, M., & Hoch, L. (1992). "Linking Children's Literature and Science Activities," *Ohio Reading Teacher* 25 (2): 13-15.

Romance, N. R., & Vitale, M. R. (1992). "A Curriculum Strategy That Expands Time for In-depth Elementary Science Instruction by Using Science-based Reading Strategies: Effects of a Year-long Study in Grade Four," *Journal of Research in Science Teaching* 29: 545-554.

Schwab, P. N., & Coble, C. R. (1985). "Reading, Thinking, and Semantic Webbing," *The Science Teacher* 52 (5): 68-71.

Shaw, D. G., & Dybdahl, C. S. (1992). "Rain Forests: Do They Hold Up the Sky?" *Preventing School Failure* 37 (1): 19-25.

Simon, S. (1982). Using Science Trade Books in the Classroom," *Science and Children* 19 (6): 5-6.

Stiffler, L. A. (1992). "A Solution in the Shelves," *Science and Children* 29 (6): 17, 46.

Tunnell, M. O., & Jacobs, J. S. (1989). "Using "Real" Books: Research Findings on Literature-based Reading Instruction," *The Reading Teacher* 42: 470-477.

GEOLOGY

Fascinating Facts for Teachers

The Study of the Earth

Geology is the study of the earth and the processes that affect it. The science of geology will be broken into three different areas for consideration. Earth materials will consider the characteristics of rocks, minerals, and fossils, as well as other earth materials of interest to elementary students. The building processes of the earth and the tearing down processes will be considered separately.

Two conflicting views of how the earth changes will be presented throughout each of the major sections. One school of thought favors the view that changes in the earth happen very slowly over a large period of time. This school, called uniformitarianism, believes that the slow processes of building and tearing down that can be seen on earth today are the same processes that operated on the earth over geologic history. That is, the processes that made rock and tore rock down have not changed over time. The same deposition of calcium carbonate that may be building limestone layers in the oceans today is the same process that built the layers of limestone found in rock strata today. The same erosional forces that can be seen sculpting the sides and bottoms of streams today are the same forces that dug the valleys of streams over geologic history. Movement of huge sections of the earth's surface that can be measured today, are driven by the same forces that adjusted crustal sections in time past. The processes have not changed, and while they are slow, they continue over huge periods of time.

Another school of thought in geology favors the view that large changes in the earth happen very suddenly in short periods of time. This view of the earth sees it as a violent place where earthquakes change the land radically, volcanoes build mountains, and huge accumulations of sediment are thrown into the air in short periods of time. It sees circular depressions with rims as impact craters from meteors and deep river gorges as originating from a single, or a series of, catastrophic floods. This viewpoint, known as catastrophism, recognizes that large scale change in the earth is due to these short-lived events that produce large scale change. Using this viewpoint, one may also argue that processes of the geologic past may have been fundamentally different than those of current time. While it is true that some students of the earth subscribe to one school of thought or another, many see value in a more eclectic view, accepting applicable parts of both schools of thought integrating them into a more reasonable picture of the dynamic nature of this planet.

Rocks, Minerals, And Earth Materials

Most earth material exposed through the soils at the earth's surface are rocks. Rocks are assemblages of two or more minerals in a hard mixture. Rarely, single minerals can be found where the mixture is not very complete, or where spaces that occur in rock have permitted mineral material to form. Minerals have five characteristics. They are 1) solid, 2) inorganic, 3) chemical compounds (or elements) with a definite chemical composition, 4) in a crystalline form (regular, repeating atomic structure), and 5) naturally occurring. In order to be classified as a mineral, the material must have the five characteristics listed above.

See Portal for Exploration "Investigating Minerals"

Minerals are solid. Water, while naturally occurring on the Earth, is not a mineral because it is not a solid. Minerals are inorganic. While coal is a solid earth material, the material of which it is made has an organic origin. Coal is made of partially decayed plant material. It was not made by any chemical process other than the partial decay of the original plant material. Therefore it is an organic earth material and not mineral. Minerals have a definite chemical composition. Random mixture of chemicals are not minerals, even if they do occur in nature. A mineral's definite chemical composition can be established through analysis and used to identify the mineral. Minerals have a crystalline form. The repeating crystalline form can grow to become a crystal, a rare find in nature. However, even "massive" samples of minerals, minerals that are not crystals, show the pattern of repeating atomic arrangement in a set of physical properties that remain the same for each mineral no matter where it is found on earth. Finally, minerals are naturally occurring. While cubic zirconia is a beautiful material, arguably as beautiful as diamond, it is manufactured and, therefore, not a mineral.

There are over 2000 identified and catalogued minerals in the world. They range from the common minerals of quartz and feldspar, to minerals more rare in nature like platinum and diamond. In some cases, like those just mentioned, the rare nature of the mineral contributes to its economic importance. With other minerals, for example bauxite and hematite, the material is not extremely rare, but these minerals serve as ores of aluminum and iron, respectively. Sometimes, the crystal forms of the mineral are found and these crystals inspire awe and wonder. The crystal-lined interior of some geodes can be beautiful as are the doubly terminated clear quartz crystals known as "Herkimer (New York) diamonds." It is a combination of physical characteristics that identifies these minerals.

A mineral's color can sometimes be used as an identification key. However, most common minerals occur in multiple colors. Quartz is a good example of this. In fact, quartz is known by other names when its color is perfect. Purple quartz, for instance, is known as amethyst. More important than color is luster, or the way a mineral reflects light. Generally, luster can be described simply as metallic or non-metallic. There are a number of kinds of non-metallic lusters (vitreous or glassy, pearlescent, dull, earthy, etc.) but most identification keys will accept simply non-metallic.

Hardness describes a mineral's resistance to being scratched. In 1820, Friedrich Mohs established a list of ten minerals which set standards used today.

See Portal for Exploration "Mohs" Scale of Hardness"

Mohs' scale of hardness, listed below, uses common minerals to establish hardness 1–10. While 1 through 9 each are harder by the same interval of hardness, diamond, number ten on the scale is much more hard than the interval would suggest. In fact, if the same interval of hardness was used to describe diamond, diamond would be over thirty on the scale with nothing between it and corundum, number nine on the scale. Therefore, for simplicity, diamond is accepted as hardness 10. A field scale of hardness, also shown below, can be used as an identification aid.

Mohs' Scale of Hardness

Mineral	Hardness Value	Field Scale
Talc	1	
Gypsum	2	
		2.5 Fingernail
Calcite	3	
		3.5 Copper penny
Fluorite	4	
Apatite	5	
		5.5 Knife blade
Feldspar	6	
		6.5 Glass
Quartz	7	
Topaz	8	
Corundum	9	
Diamond	10	

The manner in which a mineral breaks is also important. While looking at a broken area of a mineral, should multiple parallel surfaces of breakage be seen, or if the mineral breaks along a single flat surface, then the mineral is said to demonstrate cleavage. If a mineral breaks along curved surfaces, like the glass in broken bottles, it is said to demonstrate fracture.

Identifying which minerals are present in a sample is a key to identifying some rocks. However, rocks are more commonly identified by the genesis, or origin. Rocks that are made of crystalline materials that are right against each other is probably igneous. Igneous rock is formed as molten rock material below the earth's surface (magma) or on the earth's surface (lava), cools. Examples of this kind of rock include basalt, obsidian, and granite. Rock that has been formed by deposition by water or wind is called sedimentary. If the rock is made of pieces of other rock that can be seen, the rock is named for the size of those pieces. Sand-sized pieces form sandstone, mud-sized pieces form shale, and pebbles form conglomerate. Undersea chemical processes can cause the formation of sedimentary rocks called limestone and rock salt. In an undisturbed position, these rocks are found in very flat layers. Often, the pieces that make up sedimentary rock can be seen, sometimes under a magnifier, to be surrounded by a different cementing material. Sometimes the pressure and heat involved in changes to the earth's crust can cause rock to alter and form different rock from its original. This metamorphic rock often has flattened minerals or unique coloration. Examples of metamorphic rock include schist, slate, and marble. Since no new rock material is being added to the earth, rock material is simply being recycled in a rock cycle. Through processes of building and tearing down, the earth's rocks undergo many changes.

Some earth materials are not mineral, and are not, strictly speaking, rock material. Coal, being organic in nature, is not a mineral and is not a rock. However, its economic importance cannot be questioned. Hard coal (anthracite), soft coal (bituminous) and even its low grade relative, peat, are important fuels in our society. Petroleum, or crude oil, is a liquid. It is also an earth material which is not a mineral or rock. Similarly, the value of crude oil cannot be questioned. Searching for and extracting these valuable materials is an activity in which geologists are very involved.

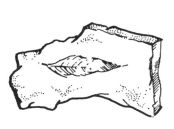 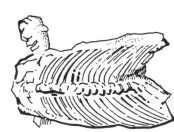 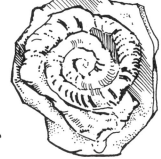

See Portal for Exploration "Making Plaster Fossils"

Any proof of pre-existing life is a fossil. This evidence can be in the form of actual remains of organisms (shark teeth or remains of sea shells) and are called original material fossils. Fossils can be shaped like the original but made of material that replaced the original as it decayed away (like limestone shaped corals or petrified wood). These types of fossils are called petrifications. A third type of fossil is the mold. It is the shape of the original organism preserved as an indentation in the rock in which it is found. Fossils can be found in sedimentary rock, rarely in metamorphic rock, and never in igneous rock. The totally new crystallization involved in the formation of igneous rock, and the heat and pressure of metamorphism, eliminates most traces of life. Some traces of life are not what one usually expects when thinking about fossils. The molds of tracks of dinosaurs in rock exposed by the erosion of a stream and the petrified solid wastes of shark found on what was once the bottoms of ancient seas are examples. In another rare site, holes in quartzite, a metamorphic rock, have been shown to be the tunnels made by worms in the sand of an ancient beach. Fossils, then, become a key to the past. They tell us a bit about the environment of the time and they can, in some cases, indicate the time that they lived.

Geologic time stretches back about four and a half billion years. Such a massive expanse of time needs to be divided into segments to ease communication. The divisions of time, called eras, given in the geologic time scale includes the Precambrian (before complex life). This era saw the development of the Earth, its atmosphere, its seas, and finally, microscopic life-forms. Some fossils of this era have been found in the shape of preserved mounds built by ancient algae. The Paleozoic (age of fishes) witnessed the development of a large array of invertebrate sea organisms. Later in this era, some of these life-forms invaded the land. The Mesozoic (age of dinosaurs) saw the rise of animal life and the dominant time of dinosaurs. Interestingly, this was also an age of unprecedented extinction. Perhaps half of all know species failed to survive this era. The Cenozoic (modern age) saw the rise of mammals as a dominant life-form. This also marks a new increase in the number of life-forms in the sea.

The presence of mankind is, arguably, three million years. We think of that as a long time, yet it represents only one fifteen hundredth of geologic time. The march of geologic time is steady, but the entire history of mankind is merely a blink in the lifetime of the earth. Evidence of life that came before mankind answers not only the question of the history of life on earth, but can also be a clue as to how we might be changing as the future unfolds. The principle that "The present is the key to the past" is a view favored in uniformitarianism while catastrophism sees the emergence of life as a more sudden event without precedence. The uniformitarianism notion is that conditions that allowed a snail to live in times past must be comparable to the conditions in which a fossil snail lived in a past era. Thus, depending on the kinds of fossils found at a place, a geologic story can unfold as to the development of that place.

Dating of fossils is a complex task. One method is absolute age dating using radioactive elements present in the volcanic ash found within, or igneous intrusions that cross, the rock strata containing the fossil. It can be assumed that the amount of radioactive material in the igneous rock decreases at a known rate. By measuring the remaining radioactivity, we can tell how long that igneous rock, and its radioactive components, have been disintegrating. Thus, the actual age of the object can be determined. Another method is relative age dating. It depends on determining the sequence of rock in an area and depends on knowing what species lived before, at the same time, and after other species. The two methods are used together to build a rather complete picture of the development of life on the Earth.

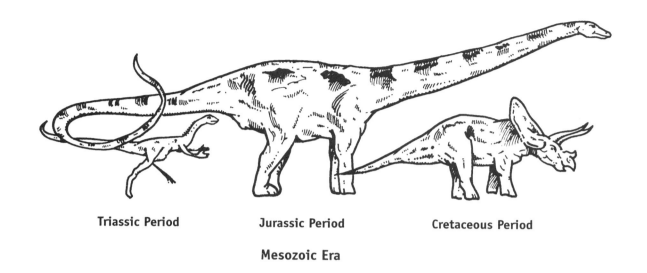

Triassic Period   **Jurassic Period**   **Cretaceous Period**

Mesozoic Era

See Portal for Exploration "Dinosaur Mystery"

One of the most interesting geologic times is the age of dinosaurs. The dinosaurs include creatures classified as saurischians whose pelvic bone arrangement resembles that of most reptiles. However, creatures classified as ornithischians have pelvic bone arrangements that resemble that of the birds. This has led to recent questions and a renewed interest in the nature and behavior of dinosaurs. A very diverse collection of creatures, all known as dinosaurs, survived as the dominant animal on the earth from 230 million years ago until 65 million years ago. Of what the dinosaurs left behind, much has been eroded away or disintegrated in the weathering process. It is interesting that so much about dinosaurs has been able to be determined, because most of the dinosaurs died and left nothing behind. That is a very large expanse of time, and rather than asking what killed the dinosaurs, perhaps we should ask why they were so successful.

Building Process of the Earth

Building processes are constantly taking place on the earth's surface. Proof of this is in the passage of time. Sufficient time has passed in geologic history that, assuming the rates of erosion on the surface have remained constant, the entire surface of the earth could have worn down to a perfectly flat surface, three times over. Something must be keeping that from happening to the surface features that we see as mountains. Over the past fifty years or so, geologists have come to realize that the earth's crust, the outer layer of the earth, is cracked into structural, or tectonic, plates. The cracked surface is like the surface of an cracked egg. These tectonic plates, less dense than the material under them, "float" on that material and are made to move about by currents in that deeper layer. The layer of the earth under the crust is called the mantle, and is plastic in nature. It flows as if it were taffy, and drags the tectonic plates around.

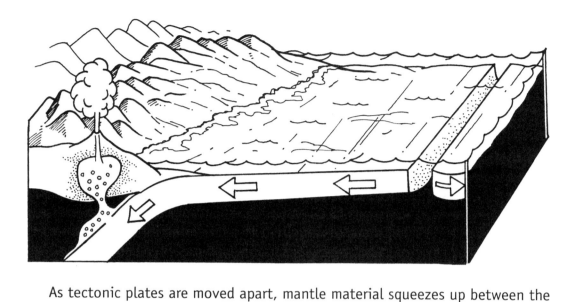

As tectonic plates are moved apart, mantle material squeezes up between the plates to form long ridges of volcanoes. This is how the longest volcano on earth, the mid-ocean ridge, has formed. At the other side of these plates, the boundaries come together. One plate may override another forcing it to dive to destruction in the hotter mantle. The destroyed plate material, being less dense than the surrounding mantle, will often float to the surface and erupt as volcanoes. These sudden eruptions are often violent as was demonstrated by the 1980 eruption of Mt. St. Helens. This is the origin of the Cascade mountain range in the north-western United States. Sometimes, the plates do not override each other, but collide without overriding. The plate material buckles upward behind the plate edge that stops moving. This process, called folding, is how the greatest mountain chains of the world have formed. The Himalayas built as the plate carrying India moved northward into the plate holding China. The Rocky Mountains have formed this way as the North American plate moves to the Pacific plate. The Alps and the Ureas have a similar origin as tectonic plate movement buckles the earth upward.

See Portal for Exploration "Folding Rocks"

All around the boundary of the tectonic plates, and anywhere within the plate where a rock unit moves in relation to another, the movement is said to create a fault. Sometimes, movement around faults is stopped as the rock units lock together. The stresses and pressures that cause the movement do not stop, and the energy is built up in the rock. At some point, the build up of energy becomes too much for the rock to resist and the rock breaks. Should the movement of the fault be sudden, the resulting release of energy can be felt as an earthquake. No area on earth is entirely safe from earthquakes, but the earthquake activity is greater around the edge of the tectonic plates. Earthquakes are measured in terms of the open-ended Richter Scale of Earthquake Magnitude. This is a measure of the amount of energy released by an earthquake. Earthquakes of magnitude of 6 and greater are known as "great earthquakes," but the damage done by an earthquake

See Portal for Exploration "Epicenter Location"

is not accurately described by this number. The modified Mercalli Scale of Earthquake Intensity is a much more accurate way of describing the actual damage done by earthquakes.

In human terms, we tend to think of volcanoes and earthquakes as disasters, and they often cause disaster. However, in terms of the earth, these movements are not disastrous. They are responsible for much of the building processes of the earth. As the plates that carry the continents about the surface of the globe change directions, changes in the frequencies of the occurrence of volcanoes and earthquakes result. Where plates butting together cease movement, the land behind buckles into huge folds. This is happening as North America moves toward the Pacific, as Asia moves toward the Pacific, and as the Pacific slowly slips under the plates around Alaska. Thus, the Pacific plate is surrounded by a zone of activity where plates are all moving in relation to each other. Thus, the region around the Pacific is tectonically active and is known as the Pacific Ring of Fire, the greatest region of tectonic activity on the globe.

Tearing Down Forces of the Earth

Just as earth processes cause a building of the earth, other forces are active that tear down the earth. The process begins as rock material is broken into smaller pieces. This process is called weathering. Weathering can have physical causes as in the repeated heating and cooling of a rock. Water is also capable of breaking the rock into smaller pieces. In frost heaving, water squeezes into cracks of rock, freezes and expands the crack as the ice is formed. The water thaws and runs deeper into the expanded crack, and freezes again. Frost heaving is a very common cause of weathering in climates that see a repeated pattern of freezing and thawing temperatures. Frost heaving is also responsible for the development of road potholes, the scourge of highways in northern climates.

Biologic material can also cause rocks to crack into smaller pieces. Lichen, a combination of moss and algae, can attach to the microscopic irregularities in a bare rock's surface. Lichen appears as a light green coating on the surface of rock materials. As the irregularities grow in size, moss, grass, and larger plants establish themselves. Growing root action has the same effect as frost heaving, but the roots literally grow deeper into the cracks of the rocks forcing the cracks to become larger. Very large rock units can be cracked in this way. It is common for someone to observe this as "a tree growing right out of a rock."

See Portal for Exploration "Chemical Weathering"

Chemical weathering is due to a chemical reaction that can occur between rock material and rain. As rain falls through air that may be polluted with sulphur or nitrogen oxides, the rain become slightly acidic. Acid rain can react with some minerals and actually break the rock as the reaction weakens target minerals. One such material is feldspar. Feldspar minerals are attacked by acid rain to make clay compounds. Thus, even granite can be made to crumble due to chemical weathering. Another example of a rock prone to chemical weathering is limestone. The limestone pyramids of Egypt have endured the ages due to the arid conditions of the climate in which they are found. However, a limestone obelisk removed from Egypt in 1879 and placed in Central Park in New York City shows remarkable loss of detail due to the ravages of the climate. Acid rain also attacks a limestone material used for building. Concrete is literally eaten away by acid rain. The surface of polished marble used as decoration on the fronts of buildings can be scarred by the chemical reactions over time.

Erosion is the movement of broken rock material by the forces of wind, water, ice, and gravity. The force of water can be tremendous as seen in events when abnormal amounts of rain have occurred, when heavy snowfalls are made to melt suddenly, or when dams are breached. During 1972, the remnants of hurricane Agnes caused extreme amounts of rainfall to swell the Susquehanna river in Pennsylvania, flooding the state capital, Harrisburg, and destroying much that was in its path. During 1996, the Mississippi was swollen to near record heights inundating vast areas of land in the Midwest. In both cases, the water moved a great amount of rock material and debris from upstream and deposited it on the downstream floodplain. Layers of mud became testament to the ability of water to convert the potential energy of the rock material from the high land areas into kinetic energy of motion as the material is moved downstream.

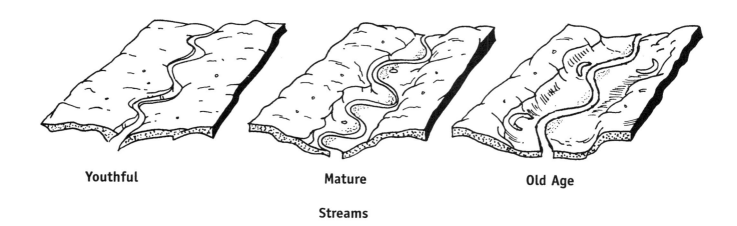

Youthful   **Mature**   **Old Age**

Streams

See Portal for Exploration "Stream Erosion"

Streams can be called youthful, mature, or old age depending on the characteristics of the stream. A stream with a high gradient (large slope) in which water moves fast through a steeply "V" shaped valley is said to be youthful. As a stream rolls large boulders down the bottom of its bed, the stream slowly wears down into the surrounding land. As time moves forward, the surrounding land wears away with the materials carried downstream and a floodplain develops. As the height of the stream falls, the velocity of the water slows, and the water begins to wear at its sides. In old age, a stream moves more slowly due to the shallow gradient over which it flows. The slow moving water does not roll large boulders over its bottom, but scours its sides with the load of sediment, small pieces of broken rocks. The path of the stream begins to cut its sides in great sweeping curves called meanders. Although the meanders begin to develop in the mature stage, old age brings steep curves that sometimes close themselves, establishing cutoffs and oxbow lakes. During flood stages, the water spills over the stream's banks and the floodplain carries the additional water. As the velocity of the water slows when the water spills over the bank, the sediment carried by the stream is deposited, first the large rocks and then the smaller ones. That is also the source of the mud that flood victims clean up, as well as the source of the rich land near rivers.

Ice is also a powerful agent of erosion. Many times over recent geologic history, the climate has become cold enough that the snow that fell during a year did not melt before the next year's snowfall began. The accumulation of snow became thick enough that the snow at the bottom of the pile turned to ice and began to flow by being squeezed outward due to its own weight. Over time, enough snow fell that a major portion of the continents were covered, and the climate became very cold. These large ice sheets, sometimes called continental glaciers, altered the landscape dramatically in several ways. First, the shear weight of the glaciers themselves crushed the rock beneath them. Today, several of these depressions now filled with water are known as the Great Lakes. The ice also carried a large amount of rock material with it. The land that glaciers moved over sometimes bears the scars of this movement with polished or scratched rock outcroppings, and, in many cases, thin soils. The region where the glaciers stop moving becomes the point at which the glacier deposits much of the rock material and debris it carried. These piles of unsorted sediment, called till, are random mixtures of sand to cobblestone to larger sizes of rock.

Currently, ice sheets cover large areas of Antarctica and Greenland, but most glaciers have retreated from the continental areas. Glaciers exist where the climate will allow the buildup of snow to continue. On most continents, advancing glaciers are limited to mountainous areas. Glaciers that are found in the mountains are called alpine glaciers, and their retreat and advance is due to

See Demonstration "Erosion by Glaciers" the same principles that cause continental ice sheets to move. In these high mountain areas, the snow builds up, the bottom snow turns to ice, and there is movement downslope due to the glacier's own weight. Similar to continental ice sheets, the alpine glacier can move tremendous amounts of rock material in front of the glacier, along its lateral margins, and down the center of the glacier. As the glacier melts, these accumulations of material are called moraines. They are named terminal moraines, lateral moraines, and medial moraines, for their former positions in the glaciers as described above, respectively.

A great deal of interest exists with regard to the effect that human activity is having on the climate. One of the areas of interest in these studies is on global temperatures. Should the global temperature rise, then it is possible for the glaciers as they exist now, to retreat. They would, literally, melt more than build. This is a concern to all of us, in that the sea level would rise and much of the population now living near the continental margins would be forced to move inland. A higher temperature is also likely to result in less solar radiation reflected by the reduced snow fields, and areas now used for growing food, like the Midwest states of the United States, may become too hot for that activity. Conversely, should human activity ultimately result in lowering the global temperature, glaciers may once again advance. The results could render large areas of land uninhabitable and alter patterns of climate dramatically. Although these would be different problems, the results would be nonetheless catastrophic.

Wind can also be a powerful agent of erosion. The size of the material that can be carried by the wind is dependent upon the wind's velocity. Most wind erosion moves silt to sand-sized particles but, although it is possible, boulder-sized material would require very high velocities. Wind is much more likely to sculpt arid regions by removing sand and leaving behind a landscape covered by larger rocks. This is called desert pavement. Blowing wind can also form sand dunes and can carve remarkable landforms as blowing sand blasts rock material away. Softer rock material is eroded by the blowing sand more easily. The wind can also remove soils loosened by over-farming. Especially when the soil is dry, the wind can completely render previously arable farmland unusable. This has happened in the midwestern United States as the dust bowl was formed in the 1930s. However, it must be remembered, that most of the spectacular erosion in deserts is not formed by the wind. The remnants of erosion standing as towers of rock in Monument Valley, Arizona, are due more to an earlier age and the action of water than to the action of wind.

Gravity is a powerful agent of erosion. In addition to the fact that it is gravity that accelerates glaciers and streams downslope, gravity can cause a great deal of havoc by its own volition. Gravity can cause unstable slopes to collapse and move downward. Mudflows are caused by water loosened and water-lubricated unstable rock masses. They can, like the one that inundated a village in Colombia during 1985, move at highway speeds and cause complete devastation of natural and man-made structures. This single event in Colombia killed 20,000 people. Creep is a downward flow of rock material and soil that can be present anywhere; a combination of water content and the slope of the land is sufficient. This slow, but persistent, movement of the landscape can often be seen as trunks of trees bend as they grow or as telephone poles are made to lean over. Rockslides usually begin as a single rock falling from a high rock face of a mountain. That single rock loosens other rocks, and they loosen other rocks, and they loosen others, and on and on. The speed of large rock slides can exceed 100 miles per hour and can move billions of cubic yards of rock material.

Landslides include a number of movements, many of which are not due to natural causes. Steep slopes caused by road cuts and attempts to increase the utility of some land areas collapse due to the instability caused by these actions. Along natural slopes, however, slumps can occur. Many Californians who have built houses along the edges of cliffs know that these slopes can become unstable during heavy rainfalls or during a phenomenon caused by earthquake. Earthquakes can jar a slope to begin a downward flow of the landscape to form a crescent-shaped depression in the cliff. The effect is much like the depression left behind as one removes a shovelful of sand from a sand pile. Many residences have been lost as the cliff near the house gave way and slumped, carrying the house with the land.

Portals for Learning: Literature

Aliki. *Digging Up Dinosaurs*. New York, NY: Harper Collins, 1988.
This *Let's Read and Find Out* book describes the types of dinosaur bones commonly found in museums as well as methods used by scientists to uncover, identify, and preserve dinosaur remains.

Arnold, C. *First Facts About the Earth*. Ladybird, 1989.
A type of junior guide, this book walks the reader through facts about our planet, its land formations, climate at different locations, rock formation, and the geology of an area. Includes a glossary and index at the end of the book.

Bains, R. *Wonders of Rivers*. Troll, 1982.
Offers the reader factual narration of the formation of rivers, their impact on the earth as they change over time, the age of rivers, and the characteristics of water movement within a river. Introduces the reader to new vocabulary about rivers.

Baylor, B. *Everybody Needs a Rock*. Aladdin, 1974.
This interesting book identifies ten rules for choosing the perfect rock for your own collection. Does not present much scientific content but would be an excellent choice for aesthetic feelings towards rocks.

Brandt, K. *Earth*. Troll, 1985.
A nonfiction story about the earth and how it changed over time, the book introduces the reader to the Paleozoic, Mesozoic, and Cenozoic Eras and describes the changes that occurred during these eras. It concludes by introducing the reader to the theory of continental drift and the results of plate stress.

Cartwright, S. *Sand*. Coward, McCann, & Geohegan, 1975.
This older book describes from where sand comes, how particle sizes differ, movement of sand, water-holding ability of sand, and various uses for sand.

Cole, J. *The Magic School Bus: Inside the Earth*. Scholastic, 1987.
This is a fictional account of Ms. Frizzle and her class as they jouney deep inside the earth to study types of rocks, how rocks and rock layers are formed, volcanoes, and rock formations such as caves.

Day, M. *Dragon in the Rocks*. Firefly Books, 1991.
A fictional account of Mary Anning's search for fossils at the Lyme Regis Cliffs in England, throughout the book, readers are introduced to the skills required for fossil collection.

Fleischman, P. *Time Train*. Harper Collins, 1991.
A teacher is nervous as a class takes a trip back in time to the prehistoric ages at Dinosaur National Monument in Utah.

Gans, R. *Danger—Iceberg*. Harper Trophy, 1964.
This *Let's Read and Find Out* book describes where icebergs originate, the natural uses such as iceberg hollows which provide shelters for polar bears, the dangers they present to ships as in the *Titanic* disaster, and their formation and eventual destruction.

Gans, R. *Rock Collecting*. Thomas Y. Crowell, 1984.
Explains the different types of rocks and minerals to readers by engaging them in the hobby of rock collecting. Provides the reader with real pictures of rocks and suggestions for keeping and maintaining a rock collection.

Gibbons, G. *Planet Earth Inside Out*. Morrow, 1995.

An excellent book that explores the earth from the "inside out," bold colorful pictures are clearly labeled which aids the reader. Covers all aspects of the physical earth, layers, continental plates, etc.

Glimmerveen, U. *A Tale of Antarctica*. Scholastic, 1989.

Conveys the tale of penguins in the Antarctica as the arrival of humans to their habitat takes its tole. The book continues to describe the change to the natural environment from the viewpoint of the penguin as the land is developed over time. Excellent book to show the environmental impact on a natural habitat.

Hiscock, B. *The Big Rock*. Atheneum, 1988.

Takes the reader on a journey about of a piece of granite located in the Adirondak Mountains of New York. Describes how continental rocks are formed, changed over time due to weathering and erosion, and are recycled. Good book for a discussion on weathering and the rock cycle.

Lewis, T. P. *Hill of Fire*. Harper and Row, 1971.

A fictional account of the eruption of the Paracutin Volcano in Mexico, this book describes the formation of the volcano as magma begins to erupt from the ground, the continued growth into a volcano, and the destruction of the village it caused.

Lyon, G. E. *Come a Tide*. Orchard Books, 1990.

An interesting book that uses colloquialism and folktale to describe what happens to a family when the river floods. Throughout the story, the grandmother tells the grandchildren that it will "come a tide" only after a certain amount of rainfall.

Peters, L. W. *The Sun, the Wind and the Rain*. Henry Holt, 1988.

This well-written story parallels a child's attempt to make a mountain of sand at the beach with the formation of the earth's mountains through natural forces and the effects of weathering from the elements on both mountains.

Simon, S. *Earthquakes*. Morrow, 1991.

An informational book that utilizes real-life photos in the explanation of earthquakes, it explains the origination of earthquakes, what causes them, and destruction that occurs.

Simon, S. *Icebergs and Glaciers*. Morrow, 1987.

Uses real-life photographs to introduce the reader to the types of glaciers and icebergs, and offers related information. Clearly introduces new vocabulary terms to the reader in a concise way while at the same time engages the reader in a well-written narrative.

Tangborn, W. V. *Glaciers*. Harper & Row, 1988.

This *Let's Read and Find Out* book takes the reader on a journey to the earth's poles in search of glaciers. After defining glaciers, the book discusses the movement of glaciers and the effects of its movement on the earth's surface. Vocabulary related to glaciers are defined throughout the story.

Zoehfeld, K. W. *How Mountains Are Made*. HarperCollins, 1995.

The *Let's Read and Find Out* book traces the formation of a mountain. It provides the reader with information on the layers of the earth, continental plate movement, resultant faulting, erosion, and weathering.

Density of Minerals

Purpose:
- Demonstrate an ability to use both the graduated cylinder and the triple beam balance.
- Compare the densities of mineral samples.

Materials Needed:
plastic graduated cylinder (100 mL)
triple beam balance
mineral samples (e.g., sulfur, talc, granite, galena)

Introduction:
This is a relatively simple lab that is meant to familiarize students with the operation of two pieces of lab apparatus—the graduated cylinder and the triple beam balance. Students will determine the density of four minerals to discover whether all minerals are of the same density.

Special Instructions:
1. Insure that all slides are at "0". If needed, zero the balance by moving the thumb screw under the pan of the balance.
2. Place the first sample on the pan of the balance.
3. Move the "100s" weight from slot to slot until the balance "trips" when the arm falls to the bottom of its range of movement. Move the weight back one slot.
4. Move the "10s" weight from slot to slot until the balance "trips" when the arm falls to the bottom of its range of movement. Move the weight back one slot.
5. Move the "units" weights until you obtain perfect balance of the pointer in the center of its range of movement.
6. Read and record this reading as the mass of the sample in the appropriate spot in the data sheet.

Procedure:
See instructions on student lab sheet.

Answer Key For Questions:
1. The increase in volume is due to the volume of the mineral alone.
2. Answers may vary. The difference represents the volume of the mineral and does not include the mass of any water that clings to the sample.
3. No

Literature Links:
Arnold, C. *Ladybird First Facts About the Earth.* Ladybird Books, 1989.
Baylor, B. *Everybody Needs a Rock.* Aladdin, 1974.
Cole, J. *The Magic School Bus: Inside the Earth.* Scholastic, 1987.
Gibbons, G. *Planet Earth Inside Out.* Morrow Junior Books, 1995.

Portals for Expansion:
Mathematics • Compare densities of rock materials to densities of common objects by creating a number line for plotting the densities determined in the lab.

Geography • Locate on a map or globe the points of origin of the rock materials being used in this lab.

Social Studies • Discuss how rock formations determined the outcome of the Battle of Gettysburg and other historical events.

Language Arts • Write a letter to a rock quarry to find out which types of rock are used for building material and which ones are used for decoration.

Density of Minerals

Procedure:
1. Measure the mass of the sample by weighing it on the balance. Record the mass on the chart below.
2. To find the volume of each sample, fill the graduated cylinder about halfway with water.
3. Measure the water in the cylinder by looking at the side and reading the number at the bottom of the meniscus. Record this number in the column "Volume Beginning." *Hint:* The meniscus is the lowest point in the top surface of the water.
4. Tilt the graduated cylinder and gently slide the mineral sample into the water.
5. Read the volume of water in the graduated cylinder. Record this number under "Volume Ending."
6. Subtract "Volume Beginning" from "Volume Ending" to find out the sample's volume. Record this number in the column "Volume of the Sample."
7. Repeat Steps 2–6 for each of the samples provided.
8. To find the density of the mineral, divide its mass by its volume. Record the number under "Density" on the chart. Complete the chart for each sample.

	Mass	Volume Beginning	Volume Ending	Volume of the Sample	Density
Sample #1					
Sample #2					
Sample #3					
Sample #4					

Questions: *Answer the questions on the back of the paper.*
1. Why is it important to measure the mass of the mineral before placing it into the water?
2. Why do you subtract "Volume Beginning" from "Volume Ending" to determine the volume of the sample?
3. Do all minerals have the same density?

Investigating Minerals

Purpose:
- Observe and record the physical properties of selected mineral samples.
- Use the physical properties to try to identify selected mineral samples.

Materials Needed:
mineral samples (e.g., quartz, calcite, halite, talc, feldspar, corundum, gypsum, apatite)
streak plate
copper penny
steel file or steel nail
glass plates
hand lens
diluted hydrochloric acid (1M)
goggles and apron
water source
triple beam balance
plastic graduated cylinder
paper toweling

Options for Lab Setup:
This investigation can be handled two different ways:
- Give each student a set of lab cards and model how to complete each task. After the demonstration, allow the students to experiment with different samples.
- Provide the equipment, materials, and lab cards at stations. Assign a different group of students to each station over several days and allow them to rotate through each station.

Procedure:
See task cards. Repeat all steps for each mineral sample.

Literature Links:
Arnold, C. *Ladybird First Facts about the Earth*. Ladybird Books, 1989.
Baylor, B. *Everybody Needs a Rock*. Aladdin, 1974.
Cole, J. *The Magic School Bus: Inside the Earth*. Scholastic, 1987.
Gans, R. *Rock Collecting*. Crowell, 1984.
Hiscock, B. *The Big Rock*. Atheneum, 1988.

Portals for Expansion:

Social Studies
- Write a report on the locations where precious and semi-precious gems are found.
- Research commercial uses of mineral materials in today's society.
- Research the issue of mines: the types, locations, need, and costs of mining.

Language Arts
- Write a narrative essay describing your favorite rock or your pet rock so that others would be able to identify it based on your description.

Investigating Minerals Lab Cards

A   **Color**

The color observed when looking at a mineral.

Observe the mineral and record its color on the data sheet.

B   **Streak**

The color of the powder of a mineral

1. Rub the mineral on the unglazed porcelain streak plate. The "streak" is the color of the powder left behind on the plate.
2. Record the color of the powder (if any) on the data sheet.
3. Record "none" for the "streak" of a mineral sample if no powder can be seen.

C   **Luster**

The way light is reflected from a mineral; metallic, glassy, or dull

1. Hold the mineral so that light strikes its surface. Observe how light is reflected.
2. If the mineral reflects light as if it were a metal, then record its luster as "metallic."
3. If the mineral reflects light as if it were glass, then record its luster as "glassy."
4. If the mineral does not reflect light well, then record its luster as "dull."

D   Breakage

The way a mineral breaks; cleavage or fracture

1. Using a magnifying glass, carefully observe a broken section of the mineral.
2. If the mineral shows a single flat surface of breakage or breaks as in a series of parallel step-like surfaces, record the breakage as "cleavage."
3. If the mineral shows curved surfaces of breakage similar to the way glass breaks, record the breakage as "fracture."

E   Hardness

Resistance to being scratched

1. Try to scratch the mineral with your fingernail. If you can, record the hardness as "less than 2.5".
2. If the mineral cannot be scratched by a fingernail but can be scratched by a copper penny, record the hardness as "between 2.5 and 3.5".
3. If the mineral cannot be scratched by a copper penny but can be scratched by a steel file or nail, record the hardness as "between 3.5 and 5.5".
4. If the mineral cannot be scratched by a steel file and cannot scratch a piece of glass, record the hardness as "between 5.5 and 7.0".
5. If the mineral can scratch glass, record the hardness as "greater than 7.0".

F   **Density**

The heft of a mineral; mass/volume

1. Find the mass of the mineral by using the triple beam balance. Record this value in the data sheet.
2. Fill the graduated cylinder about halfway with water. Record the amount of water in the cylinder.
3. Carefully slide the mineral sample into the cylinder while not allowing any water to spill out. Record the new reading.
4. Subtract the lower reading from the higher reading. Record the number as the volume of the sample.
5. Divide the mass of the sample (Step 1) by the volume of the sample (Step 4). Record this as the density of the mineral.
6. Dry the sample with a piece of paper towel.

G   **Acid Test**

The way a mineral reacts to hydrochloric acid
SAFETY NOTE: Be sure to wear the apron and goggles.
1. Place a drop of diluted hydrochloric acid on the mineral.
2. Watch for any reaction by looking for fizzing. Waft the air across the mineral to detect any odor.
3. If a reaction is observed, go to Step 8.
4. If no reaction is observed, rinse the mineral with water and then dry it with a paper towel.
5. Use a steel file to scratch the mineral to make some mineral powder on the sample.
6. Place a drop of diluted hydrochloric acid on the powder of the mineral.
7. Observe for a reaction.
8. If a reaction is observed, record a "+" in the acid test column of the data sheet.
9. If no reaction is detected, record a "-" in the acid test column.

What Is It?

Unknown mineral sample

Test the mystery sample by repeating all steps on the lab cards. Using the information collected, identify your mineral by following the steps in the dichotomous mineral key:

1. a. Mineral is metallic. (Go to Step 2.)
    b. Mineral is nonmetallic. (Go to Step 5.)
2. a. Mineral looks like gold. (pyrite)
    b. Mineral looks gray, black, or silver. (Go to Step 3.)
3. a. Mineral reacts to HCl with rotten egg oder. (galena)
    b. Mineral has no reaction or a reaction with no oder. (Go to Step 4.)
4. a. Mineral streak is brown-red. (hematite)
    b. Mineral streak is gray-black. (magnetite)
5. a. Mineral reacts to HCl. (Go to Step 6.)
    b. Mineral does not react to HCl. (Go to Step 7.)
6. a. Acid bubbles and fizzes on mineral's surface. (calcite)
    b. Acid bubbles and fizzes on powder of mineral. (dolomite.)
7. a. Mineral is harder than steel. (Go to Step 8.)
    b. Mineral is softer than steel. (Go to Step 15.)
8. a. Mineral demonstrates cleavage. (Go to Step 9.)
    b. Mineral demonstrates fracture. (Go to Step 11.)
9. a. Mineral is dark gray or black. (hornblende.)
    b. Mineral is light colored. (Go to Step 10.)
10. a. Mineral is harder than glass. (topaz)
    b. Mineral is softer than glass. (feldspar)
11. a. Mineral has colorless streak. (Go to Step 12.)
    b. Mineral has red-brown streak. (hematite)
12. a. Mineral is glassy. (Go to Step 13.)
    b. Mineral is not glassy. (Go to Step 14.)
13. a. Mineral is green. (olivine)
    b. Mineral is not green. (quartz)
14. a. Mineral fractures (crumbles) easily. (garnet)
    b. Mineral is very hard to break. (corundum)
15. a. Mineral is bright yellow. (sulfur)
    b. Mineral is other than bright yellow. (Go to Step 16.)
16. a. Mineral cleaves in thin, pliable sheetsg (Go to Step 17.)
    b. Mineral doesn't cleave in thin sheets. (Go to Step 18.)
17. a. Mineral is light colored. (muscovite)
    b. Mineral is dark colored. (biotite)
18. a. Mineral feels like soap or is greasy. (talc)
    b. Mineral doesn't feel greasy or like soap. (Go to Step 19.)
19. a. Mineral is white or gray. (gypsum)
    b. Mineral is dark gray, black or brown. (amphibole)

Physical Characteristics of Minerals Data Sheet

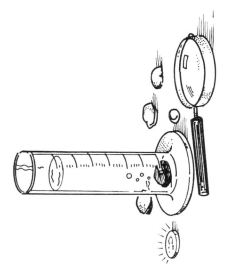

Mineral Name	Color	Streak	Luster	Breakage	Hardness	Density	Acid Test	Comment

Using Mohs' Scale of Hardness

Purpose: • Identify each of the minerals of Mohs' Scale of Mineral Hardness from 1 to 9.
• Apply the principle of hardness in the identification of an unknown mineral sample.

Materials Needed: mineral samples (e.g., talc, gypsum, calcite, fluorite, apatite, feldspar, quartz, topaz, corundum)
any other sample of the above with a color difference
steel file or steel nail
piece of glass
lid of shoe box

Introduction: Place the nine unmarked mineral samples in the lid of a shoe box. A tenth sample is marked "unknown." The nine samples represent hardness values 1 through 9 on Mohs' Scale of Hardness. The students will unscramble the samples and arrange them in order of hardness by following the procedure on the lab sheet. When finished, the students will use the "Known Hardness Collection" to identify the unknown mineral for the lab sheet "How Hard Is It?" on page 45.

Procedure: *Safety Note:* Tape the edges of the glass to prevent injuries.
See instructions on student lab sheet.

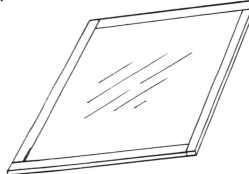

Answer Key: **Scale of Hardness:**
Hardness 1—talc
Hardness 2—gypsum
Hardness 3—calcite
Hardness 4—fluorite
Hardness 5—apatite
Hardness 6—feldspar
Hardness 7—quartz
Hardness 8—topaz
Hardness 9—corundum

Questions:
1. The hardness of a mineral or its resistance to being scratched
2. Scratched

Literature Links: Arnold, C. *Ladybird First Facts About the Earth.* Ladybird Books, 1989.
Baylor, B. *Everybody Needs a Rock.* Aladdin, 1974.
Cole, J. *The Magic School Bus: Inside the Earth.* Scholastic, 1987.
Gans, R. *Rock Collecting.* Crowell, 1984.
Hiscock, B. *The Big Rock.* Atheneum, 1988.

Portals for Expansion: **Social Studies**
• Write a report describing the origin and value of a precious or semi-precious earth material.

Mathematics
• Create a number line to plot the hardness of a variety of mineral and non-mineral materials.

Using Mohs' Scale of Hardness

HARDNESS 1: _____ ◯

HARDNESS 2: _____ ◯

HARDNESS 3: _____ ◯

HARDNESS 4: _____ ◯

HARDNESS 5: _____ ◯

HARDNESS 6: _____ ◯

HARDNESS 7: _____ ◯

HARDNESS 8: _____ ◯

HARDNESS 9: _____ ◯

Known Hardness Collection

Procedure:
1. Scratch each sample with your fingernail.
   • For those that you can scratch, follow Step 2.
   • Set all others aside for Step 3.
2. Those samples that you can scratch represent Hardness Values 1 and 2. Scratch one sample against the other and determine which one can be scratched and which one can do the scratching. Place the samples in the corresponding circles:
   • The one that is scratched is Hardness 1.
   • The one doing the scratching is Hardness 2.

3. Scratch the seven remaining samples with a piece of glass.
   - Those that can be scratched by the glass represent Hardness Values 3, 4, and 5. Use these three samples in Step 4.
   - Set all others aside for Step 5.
4. Work with the samples that can be scratched by glass. Scratch one against the other, two at a time, to determine which one is the hardest mineral of the group. *Remember:* It will be the one that can scratch the other two samples. Place the samples in the corresponding circles:
   - Identify the sample which is the softest. (It will be the one that is scratched by the other minerals.) This one is Hardness 3.
   - Identify the sample which is the hardest. This one is Hardness 5.
   - Place the remaining sample in Hardness 4.
5. Scratch the four remaining samples with a steel file or nail.
   - The one that can be scratched by a file is Hardness 6.
   - Set all others aside for Step 6.
6. The three remaining minerals represent Hardness Values 7 through 9. Scratch one against the other, two at a time, to determine which one is the hardest mineral of the group. Place the samples in the corresponding circles:
   - Identify the sample which is the softest. (It will be the one that is scratched by the other minerals.) This one is Hardness 7.
   - Identify the sample which is the hardest. This one is Hardness 9.
   - Place the remaining sample in Hardness 8.
7. Check to be sure all minerals are placed in their proper locations on the lab sheet. Check the answers with your teacher. Record the names of the samples on the lab sheet.

Questions: 1. What characteristic of a mineral is described by its hardness?

2. Hardness can be described as the resistance of a mineral to being _____.

LAB
Geology

How Hard Is It?

Determining the hardness of an unknown mineral sample.

Here is your opportunity to act like a geologist. First, ask your teacher for the mystery sample. Use what you know about Moh's Scale of Hardness to identify the sample's hardness value. You will need to use your "Known Hardness Collection."

Procedure:

1. Scratch the mineral with your fingernail.
   - If it cannot be scratched, then go to Step 3.
   - If the unknown is scratched by the fingernail, go to Step 2.
2. Scratch the unknown against Numbers 1 and 2 in your "Known Hardness Collection." Determine whether it is Hardness Value 1 or 2. *Remember:* Value 2 will scratch talc, and Value 1 will be scratched by gypsum.
   - Identify the Hardness Value for the unknown as 1 or 2.
3. Determine if the unknown can scratch glass.
   - If it does, go to Step 5.
   - If the unknown cannot scratch glass, go to Step 4.
4. Scratch the unknown by Numbers 3, 4, and 5 in your "Known Hardness Collection."
   - If the unknown is Hardness Value 3, known samples 4 and 5 will scratch it.
   - If the unknown is Hardness Value 5, neither known samples 3 nor 4 will be able to scratch it.
   - If the unknown is Hardness Value 4, then known sample 3 will be scratched by the unknown. However, the unknown will be scratched by known sample 5.
   - Identify the Hardness Value for the unknown as 3, 4, or 5.
5. Scratch the unknown with a steel file.
   - If the steel file can scratch the unknown, then it is Hardness Value 6.
   - If the file cannot scratch the mineral, then go to Step 7.
6. Scratch the unknown by Numbers 7, 8, and 9 in your "Known Hardness Collection."
   - If the unknown is Hardness Value 7, known samples 8 and 9 will scratch it.
   - If the unknown is Hardness Value 9, neither known samples 7 nor 8 will be able to scratch it.
   - If the unknown is Hardness Value 8, then known sample 7 will be scratched by the unknown. However, the unknown will be scratched by known sample 9.
7. Present the unknown to your teacher labeled with the answer you have determined.

Continental Puzzle

Purpose:
- Assemble a model of the supercontinent Pangea by fitting together a map of the current continents.
- Suggest reasons why the map does not now fit together with 100% accuracy.

Materials Needed:
map of the continents (page 48)
construction paper
school glue
scissors
large map of the world

Procedure: See instructions on student lab sheet.

Answer Key For Questions:
1. No, not exactly. There are overlapping areas and other areas that show gaps.
2. Yes. Answers will vary. Continental material may have been formed (e.g., volcanoes) following the breakup of Pangea.
3. Yes. Answers will vary. Continental material may have been eroded (e.g., shorelines) following the breakup of Pangea.

Literature Links:
Arnold, C. *Ladybird First Facts about the Earth*. Ladybird Books, 1989.
Brandt, K. *Earth*. Troll, 1985.
Cole, J. *The Magic School Bus: Inside the Earth*. Scholastic, 1987.
Gibbons, G. *Planet Earth Inside Out*. Morrow Junior Books, 1995.
Zoehfeld, K. W. *How Mountains Are Made*. HarperCollins, 1995.

Portals for Expansion:
Mathematics
- Determine by ratios size comparisons of the continents.
- Estimate the accuracy of fit by estimating the area of the supercontinent assembled and estimating the area of overlap and gaps using graph paper for the continents.

Science
- Compare fossil remains on edges of continental plates and draw conclusions.

Language Arts
- Develop a persuasive argument to use in a debate regarding the evidence for or against Pangea.

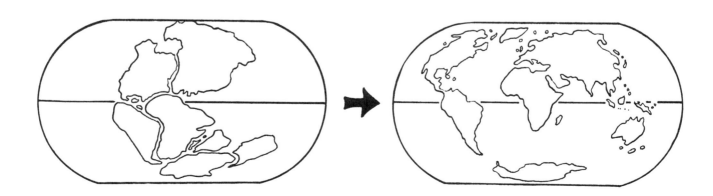

Continental Puzzle

Procedure: 1. As carefully as possible, cut out each of the continents on the map provided.
2. Place the continent shapes on a piece of paper in the arrangement they now have on the globe's surface. If needed, refer to the world map.
3. Millions of years ago the continents formed one supercontinent called Pangea. Since that time the continents have moved to their present positions following the breakup of Pangea. Reverse this process and try to fit the continents together as one huge continent.
4. Do not move the continents through or across each other. They may be moved in straight lines, rotated, or in large arcs.
5. When you find what you believe is the "best fit," glue the pieces in place on a dark piece of construction paper.

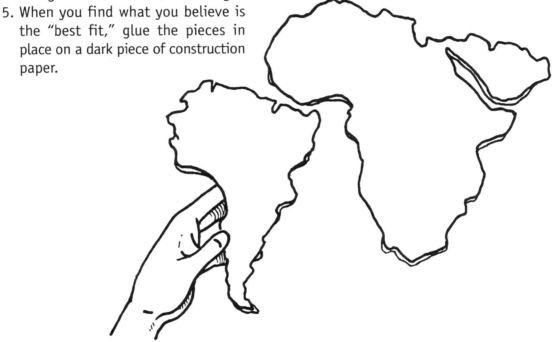

Questions: 1. Do the continents fit exactly together?

2. Do you have places where the continents overlap? What may cause this overlap?

3. Do you have places where the continents have gaps between them? What may cause these gaps?

Continental Map Pattern

Folding Rocks

Purpose:
- Construct a model of folded rock layers.
- Identify the "up folds" as anticlines and the "down folds" as synclines.
- Define how eroded anticlines and eroded synclines can be identified by the age of rock layers.

Materials Needed:
four colors of modeling clay
rolling pin or wooden dowel
two large wooden blocks (51 mm x 102 mm x 203 mm)
one piece of plywood (3 mm x 152 mm x 152 mm)
one plastic knife

Procedure: See instructions on student lab sheet.

Answer Key For Questions:
1. Along the center axis of the fold
2. Older. Answers will vary. Upfolds bring older rock to the surface along the center axis of the fold.

Literature Links:
Arnold, C. *Ladybird First Facts About the Earth*. Ladybird Books, 1989.
Brandt, K. *Earth*. Troll, 1985.
Cole, J. *The Magic School Bus: Inside the Earth*. Scholastic, 1987.
Gibbons, G. *Planet Earth Inside Out*. Morrow Junior Books, 1995.
Peters, L.W. *The Sun, the Wind and the Rain*. Henry Holt, 1988.
Zoehfeld, K.W. *How Mountains Are Made*. HarperCollins, 1995.

Portals for Expansion:

Language Arts
- Write an essay describing the sequence of events in the building of the Alps or another major folded mountain chain.

Art
- Create a drawing or papier-mâché model of folded mountains.
- Using *Planet Earth Inside Out* by Gibbons, create a wall mural to represent the stages of mountain formation.

Folding Rocks

Procedure:

1. Make a flat "pancake" from one color of modeling clay. Set this aside. This "pancake" represents the oldest rock layer.
2. To represent the younger rock layers, make three more clay "pancakes" in different colors.
3. Stack the clay "pancakes" one on top of the other in an alternating pattern—the oldest layer on the bottom, the youngest layer on top.
4. Place wooden blocks on either side of the stack of clay "pancakes."
5. Squeeze the clay by moving the blocks slowly together. When the blocks are close enough together, place the plywood across the top of the blocks.

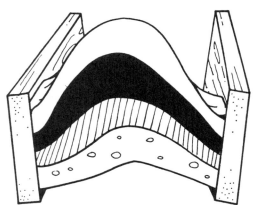

6. Continue to squeeze the blocks together while holding the plywood cover down.
7. When the blocks are too hard to move, remove the plywood cover and the blocks.
8. Make a vertical cut through the clay using the plastic knife.
9. On the back of this paper, draw a picture of the layers of clay as they are revealed by the fresh cut. Label the colors.
   - Places where the layers of clay are pushed upward are called **anticlines.** Label each anticline as you see it in your picture with a circled letter "A."
   - Places where the layers of clay are pushed downward are called **synclines.** Label each syncline as you see it in your picture with a circled letter "S."
10. Make a horizontal cut to remove the top half of the clay.
11. Make a second drawing, viewed from the top. Instead of labeling the clay according to color, label it according to "oldest," "old," "young," and "youngest."
    - Label where you had identified each anticline with a circled letter "A."
    - Label where you had identified each syncline with circled letter "S."

Questions:

1. When rock units squeeze together, deeply buried layers of rock get folded. Describe where the older rock (the color that was on the bottom) ended up after the rocks were folded.

2. Are the cores of folded mountains older or younger than surrounding rock layers? Explain your answer.

Epicenter Location

Purpose:
- Apply the relationship of P-wave (longitudinal or primary wave) and S-wave (transverse or secondary wave) speeds to estimate the time of arrival of S waves at three seismic stations.
- Apply the ratio of distance traveled to P-wave arrival time to estimate distances from three seismic stations.
- Use the distances from the three seismic stations to triangulate the location of the epicenter.

Materials Needed:
map
data sheet
drawing compass with pencil

Special Instructions: Since no measurement is exact, a "triangle of uncertainty" is where the epicenter lies. Have each student darken the "triangle of uncertainty" described as that area inside all three circles.

Procedure: See student lab sheet for instructions.

Answer Key For Questions:
1. Southeastern region of the continent
2. Three
3. Answers will vary. For example: The two circles will intersect at two points. The third circle establishes which intersection is the area of high probability.

Literature Links:
Brandt, K. *Earth*. Troll, 1985.
Simon, S. *Earthquakes*. Morrow Junior Books, 1991.

Web Site Link: **Virtual Earthquake**
http://vflylab.calstatela.edu/edesktop/VirtApps/VirtualEarthQuake/VQuakeIntro.html
This simulation provides lots of practice in looking at seismograms and identifying the epicenter of an earthquake. Students can choose the location for the test earthquake.

Portals for Expansion: **Language Arts**
- Write a story that explains what you would feel and experience if a major earthquake were to strike your town today.

Social Studies
- Research how many earthquakes have affected your town/city/state/region in history.
- Interview city/state/Red Cross officials regarding the readiness of your community for major earthquakes.

Name _____

Epicenter Location

Procedure:
1. Convert the arrival time of P waves to seconds. Record this time in the data sheet.
2. Since P waves move at 6 kilometers per second, multiply the number of seconds by 6. Record this as the distance from the epicenter using P wave arrival time.
3. S waves move at half the speed of P waves and, therefore, take twice as long to get to each station. Double the arrival times (in seconds) and record in the appropriate space.
4. Convert the arrival time of the S wave to mixed units by dividing by 60. The remainder from the long division is the number of seconds.
5. To plot the earthquake epicenter on the map of the Lost Continent, the scale distance for the map must be calculated. Copy the "Distance from the Epicenter Using P-wave Time" from your own figures in the "Earthquake Event Data" chart to the "Distances to be Plotted on the Map" chart.
6. Divide the distance by 250 km per inch (100 km per cm) in order to find out what measurement on the map represents scale distance to the epicenter.
7. Set a drawing compass to the scale measurement and draw as much of a circle around each station as is possible given the size of the paper.
8. The point that all circles come together is the epicenter.

Earthquake Event Data

Seismic Station	P-wave Arrival Time (mixed units)	P-wave Arrival Time (seconds)	Distance from Epicenter Using P-wave Time	S-wave Arrival Time (seconds)	S-wave Arrival Time (mixed units)
Hightown	2 min., 29 sec.				
Beach City	1 min., 24 sec.				
Metropolis	2 min., 47 sec.				

Distances to be Plotted on the Map

Seismic Station	Distance from Epicenter Using P-wave Time	Distance Represented to Map Scale
Hightown		
Beach City		
Metropolis		

LAB
Geology

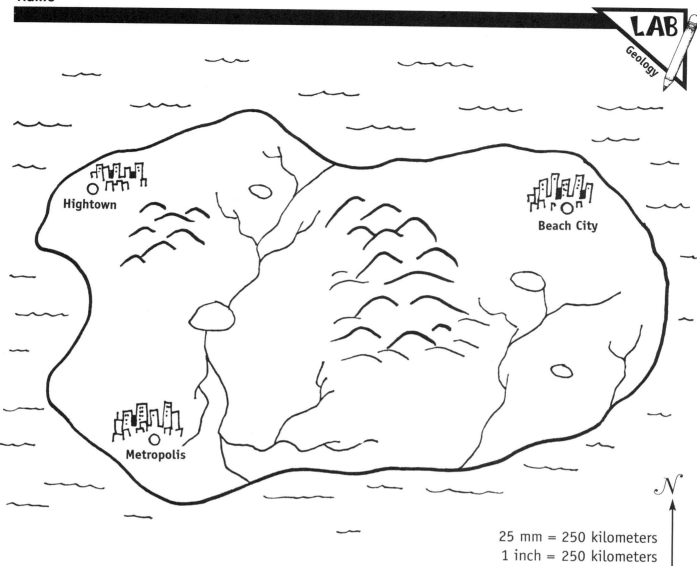

Hightown

Beach City

Metropolis

25 mm = 250 kilometers
1 inch = 250 kilometers

$\mathcal{N}$

Questions: 1. Describe where the epicenter is in terms of the shape of the Lost Continent.

2. How many seismic stations are necessary to plot the location of an epicenter?

3. What is the problem in trying to locate an epicenter with only two seismic stations?

Chemical Weathering

Purpose:
- Compare the effectiveness of chemical weathering in normal water and water that is slightly acid.
- Use lab equipment to measure the differences in the two examples of weathering.

Materials Needed:
limestone chips
two 2-liter plastic bottles
screens for rinsing the limestone chips
diluted hydrochloric acid (1M)
goggles and apron
triple beam balance
pan

Procedure: See instructions on student lab sheet.

Answer Key For Questions:
1. Acid water
2. Answers may vary. For example: Limestone will last longer in dry climates. Chemical weathering happens when acid rainwater clings to the limestone surface.
3. Answers may vary. For example: Limestone monuments last longer in Egypt because the climate is dry. There is less chance for acid water to attack the limestone.
4. No. Answers may vary. For example, acid water attacks more kinds of minerals more effectively than ordinary water.

Literature Links:
Arnold, C. *Ladybird First Facts About the Earth*. Ladybird Books, 1989.
Brandt, K. *Earth*. Troll Associates, 1985.
Cartwright, S. *Sand*. Coward, McCann, & Geohegan, 1975.
Cole, J. *The Magic School Bus: Inside the Earth*. Scholastic, 1987.
Hiscock, B. *The Big Rock*. Atheneum, 1988.
Peters, L. W. *The Sun, the Wind and the Rain*. Henry Holt, 1988.
Zoehfeld, K. W. *How Mountains Are Made*. HarperCollins, 1995.

Portals for Expansion:

Social Studies
- Write letters to local, state/province, or national historical societies asking them for pictures of statues that you can compare to original or recent photographs.
- Students can take a field trip to a cemetery to examine the degree of weathering to the dates given on headstones.

Language Arts
- Write letters to national parks asking how weathering is evident in geologic and built structures in the parks.
- Write a letter to an operator of cave tours to find out how weathering contributed to the formation of the caves.

Mathematics
- Compare the acid rain in urban, suburban, and rural areas with data you can obtain from your state department of environmental resources.

Chemical Weathering

Procedure: *Preparation*

1. Into one plastic bottle, place 250 mL of water.
2. Into the other plastic bottle, place 150 mL of water and 100mL of diluted hydrochloric acid. *Note:* Be sure to wear the safety goggles and apron.

Measuring the limestone chips

3. Set the triple beam balance for 200 grams.
4. Set a paper towel on the triple beam balance pan. Carefully pour limestone chips onto a paper towel until the balance "trips" and the arm moves.
5. Add or take away limestone until the triple beam balance is nearly balanced.
6. Use the units slide to exactly measure the mass of the limestone. Record the mass on the plain water data sheet.
7. Make a second pile of limestone using Steps 3 through 5. Use the units slide to exactly measure the mass of the limestone. Record the mass on the acid water data sheet.

The plain water test

8. Begin to time for ten minutes as you pour the appropriate limestone into the bottle of plain water. When all of the limestone is in the bottle, secure the cap, and shake the bottle for what remains in the ten minutes.
9. At the end of the ten minutes, pour the contents onto the screen placed over a pan to catch the water. Add water to the bottle to rinse out any remaining chips.
10. Rinse the limestone with plain water to carry wet dust away. Towel dry this rock material and set it aside to air-dry. Label it as limestone from plain water.

The acid water test

11. Begin to time for another ten minutes by pouring the appropriate limestone into the bottle of acid water. When all of the limestone is in the bottle, secure the cap and shake the bottle for what remains in the ten minutes.
12. At the end of the ten minutes, pour the contents onto the screen placed over a pan to catch the water. Add water to the bottle to rinse out any remaining chips.
13. Rinse the limestone with plain water to carry wet dust and acid water away. Towel dry this rock material and set it aside to air-dry. Label it as limestone from acid water.

The results

14. After the plain water rock chips are dry, carefully pour them onto a paper towel on the pan of a triple beam balance, then find the mass.
15. Record this in the appropriate space on the Data Sheet below.
16. Repeat Step 14 above and find the mass of the limestone from acid water.
17. Record this in the appropriate space on the data sheet.
18. Calculate the difference between the mass of the limestone before and after it is shaken in plain or acid water.

Data Sheet

Plain Water	
Beginning mass of limestone:	
Ending mass of limestone:	
Mass lost to weathering:	

Acid Water	
Beginning mass of limestone:	
Ending mass of limestone:	
Mass lost to weathering:	

Questions: *Answer the questions on the back of the paper.*

1. Is plain or acid water more effective in weathering rock?
2. Do you think limestone will last longer in dry climates or in rainy climates?
3. Explain why limestone monuments last longer in Egypt than in New York City.
4. Will monuments last longer in regions that have more acid rainfall? Explain.

Stream Erosion

Purpose:
- Observe the action of moving water on sand landscapes in a stream table.
- Identify places that demonstrate erosion, deposition, deltas, side-cutting, down-cutting, meanders, cutoffs, and oxbow lakes.
- Explain how the incline of the stream table affects the rates of erosion, and characteristics of the streams generated.

Materials Needed:
stream table
water
sand

Procedure:
See instructions on student lab sheet.

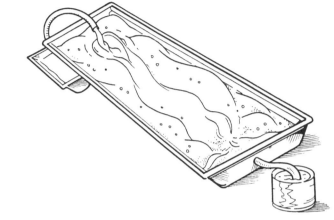

Data Chart:

	Youthful	Mature	Old-age Streams
Cutting:	bottom	both	side
Pathway:	straight	crooked	severely crooked
Velocity:	high	moderate	low
Meanders	none	some development	well developed
Cut-offs	none	none	well developed
Oxbow lakes	none	none	well developed
Location of deposits	mouth	inside of curves	inside of curves

Literature Links:
Bains, R. *Wonders of Rivers*. Troll, 1982.
Lyon, G. E. *Come a Tide*. Orchard Books, 1990.

Portals for Expansion:

Social Studies
- Interview city/state/Red Cross officials regarding the readiness of your community for major flood events.
- Research recent major flood events that have occurred near your town/state.

Language Arts
- Write a poem or other work that describes your feelings after watching a video of flood damage.
- Invite a speaker from the Army Corps of Engineers to speak on the topic of flood control.

Art
- Create a model of a river or stream that demonstrates the effect of dam construction.

Mathematics
- Contact the dam operator for a dam in your region or state. Find out the volume held by the dam. Calculate the weight of water held back.

Stream Erosion

Setup:

1. Place sand in the stream table and bank it toward what will become the elevated end of the stream table. The bottom third of the table should be bare.
2. Attach a drain tube to the bottom of the tray. Put the tube into a can in a sink so that the water flows into the can and then into the sink. Any sand in the water flow will be caught in the can.

Procedure:

Youthful Streams – Trial A

1. Elevate one end of the stream table about 30 cm.
2. Using a drip tray, begin a flow of water into the stream table so that the water strikes the sand gently and over a larger area.
3. Observe the route and velocity that the water takes as it flows through the sand to the bottom of the stream table.
4. Describe the path of the streams that form in this model. Record whether the streams erode more toward their sides or more down at the bottom of their channels.
5. Observe any deposition that might be taking place at the bottom end of the stream.
6. Stop the flow of water and push the sand evenly back toward the elevated end of the stream table. Record all information on the data chart.

Mature Streams – Trial B

7. Decrease the height of the elevated end of the stream table to 20 cm.
8. Begin the flow of water. (See Step 2.)
9. Observe the shape of the streams that form and the velocity of water through the stream channels in comparison to the earlier streams.
10. Describe the path of the streams that form in this model, and whether the streams erode more toward their sides or more down at the bottom of their channels.
11. Observe the formation of meanders in this model.
12. Observe areas of deposition. Look at any steep turns that develop in the stream and at the end of the stream.
13. Stop the flow of water and push the sand evenly back toward the elevated end of the stream table. Record all information on the data chart.

Old-age Streams – Trial C

14. Decrease the height of the elevated end of the stream table to 10 cm.
15. Begin the flow of water. (See Step 2.)
16. Observe the shape of the streams that form and the velocity of water through the stream channels in comparison to the earlier streams.
17. Describe the path of the streams that form in this model. Record whether the streams erode more toward their sides or more down at the bottom of their channels.
18. Observe the formation of meanders, cutoffs, and oxbow lakes.

19. Observe any deposition that may be taking place at steep turns in the path of the streams and at the bottom ends of the streams. Look especially for the formation of a delta.
20. Observe the path of water as it passes through the delta. Observe to see if the water always runs on the same channel.
21. Record all information on the data chart.

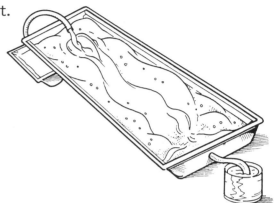

Stream Table Data Chart

	Youthful Streams	Mature Streams	Old-age Streams
Height of the Stream Table			
Bottom-or Side-Cutting			
Pathways of Streams			
Velocity of Streams			
Presence of Meanders			
Presence of Cut-offs			
Presence of Oxbow Lakes			
Location of Deposition			

Erosion by Glaciers

Teacher Demonstration

Purpose:
- Explain how rock particles embedded in moving ice are responsible for most glacial erosion.
- Identify types of evidences that glaciers have been involved in erosion.
- Speculate on factors that can affect the rates of erosion by glacial action.

Materials Needed:
very large tray
large soap bars
sand and pebble mixture
ice cubes

Setup: To prepare for the activity, cut the soap into thin slices. Chill the slices to ensure that the soap will be hard, not soft and sticky.

Procedure:
1. On the bottom of the tray, arrange the soap slices to cover one end.
2. Cover the rest of the tray with the sand and pebble mixture.
3. While pushing down on an ice cube, move the ice cube across the sand and pebble mixture to and across the soap slices.
4. Observe the bottom side of the ice cube.
5. Observe the top side of the soap slices.

Questions for Discussion:
1. What changes did you observe in the bottom surface of the ice from the beginning of the demonstration to the end of the demonstration? (*Answers will vary. For example, grit has become embedded into the ice.*)
2. What is the shape of the path left by the ice? Are the sides of the path steep like a "U" or shallow like a "V"? (*"U"*)
3. What is the evidence left behind on the surface of the soap that the model of a glacier had passed? (*Answers will vary. For example, grit has carved striations [scratches] on the soap.*)
4. Would the results differ if there was a change to the amount of downward pressure exerted on the ice? (*Yes. Answers will vary. For example, striation would be deeper.*)
5. What evidence in real rocks can be found that a glacier had passed? (*Striation.*)
6. How would repeated advances and retreats by glaciers affect the geology of a region? (*Answers will vary. Some examples of glacial movement includes: repeated carving of the topography; multiple layers of striations; debris [till] pushed to different locations.*)

Literature Links:
Gans, R. *Danger—Iceberg*. Harper Trophy, 1964.
Glimmerveen, U. *A Tale of Antarctica*. Scholastic, 1989.
Simon, S. *Icebergs and Glaciers*. Morrow Junior Books, 1987.
Tangborn, W. V. *Glaciers*. Harper & Row, 1988.

Portals for Expansion:
Social Studies • Research to find out if glacial deposits/erosion have impacted the economy or history of the region.
Mathematics • Measure the depth of the scratches made in the soap and graph them in relation to the pressure exerted on the ice.

Making Plaster Fossils

Purpose:
- Explain how fossils are formed.
- Define the three types of fossils using products formed in the demonstration.

Materials Needed:
plastic fossil models or other objects
modeling clay
plaster of Paris
nonstick cooking spray
unsharpened pencils

Procedure: See instructions on student lab sheet.

Answer Key For Questions:
1. Original material fossil
2. Mold fossil
3. No
4. Mold fossil and original fossil

Literature Links:
Aliki. *Digging Up Dinosaurs*. HarperCollins, 1988.
Day, M. *Dragon in the Rocks*. Firefly Books, 1991.
Fleischman, P. *Time Train*. HarperCollins, 1991.

Portals for Expansion:
Language Arts
- Describe an environment in which you believe that your fossil could survive.
- Using the old nursery rhyme "She sells sea shells . . . ," describe how this relates to the story about Mary Anning. (The nursery rhyme was based in part on Mary Anning's sales of shells to fund her studies.)

Making Plaster Fossils

Procedure:

1. Make two clay "pancakes" from modeling clay.
2. Select a plastic fossil model. Lightly coat it with nonstick cooking spray.
3. Lay the fossil model on one of the pancakes.
4. Place an unsharpened pencil on the pancake so that the unsharpened end touches the fossil model and the other end extends off the pancake.
5. Press the pencil and the fossil model into the clay.
6. Cover the model and pencil with the second pancake. Press the second "pancake" so that the fossil model and the pencil are imprinted on the inside of the pancakes.
7. Carefully open the pancakes sufficiently to remove the fossil model and the pencil.
8. Make sure that there is a smooth path between the shape of the pencil and the shape of the plastic fossil that is preserved in the clay.
9. Close the two pancakes together and seal the edges. Carefully press the pancakes together around the location of the plastic fossil and pencil molds.
10. Open into a funnel shape that end of the pencil mold that can be seen on the edge of the clay "pancakes."
11. Carefully pour prepared plaster of Paris into the mold, then allow it to harden.
12. After time has passed, open the pancakes to find the plaster form of the fossil.
13. Identify the fossils as follows:
    - The shape of the fossil preserved in the clay is called a **mold fossil.**
    - The original bone or shell (or plastic) of the organism is called an **original material fossil.**
    - The shape of the original preserved but with different material is called a **petrification.**

Questions:

1. If an actual shark's tooth is found in a sand deposit, what kind of fossil is it?

2. If an empty outline of a snail shell is found in a rock, what kind of fossil is it?

3. Are the trees in the Petrified Forest of Arizona made of wood?

4. Which two types of fossils might you be able to find at the same time at the same place and of the same thing?

Dinosaur Mystery

Purpose:
- Build and describe in writing the "creature" formed with sugar cubes.
- Explain why investigating the physical features of dinosaurs is a difficult task.

Materials Needed:

24 sugar cubes
silicon sealant
1-liter container of water
small container (coffee-can sized) of sand
  (make small drainage holes in the bottom of can)

aluminum foil
dishpan
spoons

Procedure: See instructions on student lab sheet.

Behind the Scenes: Silicone sealant needs to be used as a glue because it is not a water-based adhesive and there-fore will not dissolve the sugar cubes. You can find silicone sealant in the hardware aisle of most stores.

Answer Key For Questions:
1. Answers will vary. Examples: Some sand stuck to the sugar where none was expected. Some sugar dissolved where there was some originally.
2. Answers will vary. See above for examples.
3. Answers will vary. See above for examples.
4. Answers will vary. For example, the paleontologist makes educated guesses regarding the shape of the original material.

Literature Links:
Aliki. *Digging Up Dinosaurs*. HarperCollins, 1988.
Day, M. *Dragon in the Rocks*. Firefly Books, 1991.
Fleischman, P. *Time Train*. HarperCollins, 1991.

Web Site Link:
Dinosaurs in Cyberspace: Dinolinks
http://www.ucmp.berkeley.edu/diapsids/dinolinks.html
This website links students to other sites, covering topics which range from fossils and exhibits to stories and clubs.

Portals for Expansion:
Language Arts
- Write a descriptive paragraph about the dinosaur you have created. Give the dinosaur a scientific name that describes the dinosaur using Latin scientific roots, prefixes, and suffixes.

Art
- Create a diorama using your dinosaur and materials from nature.

Mathematics
- Using square foot floor tiles, students can measure the dimensions of actual dinosaurs.
- Research and then compare the strides and walking rates of several dinosaur species.
- Using a graph, compare the length of dinosaur femurs and their overall heights to determine if a relationship exists.

Science
- Compare the environment in which you live to the environment of a variety of dinosaurs to determine which dinosaur would make the best pet.

Dinosaur Mystery

Procedure:

1. Working on aluminum foil, create a dinosaur shape with 12 sugar cubes. Use the silicon sealant to glue the pieces together.
2. Draw your dinosaur, then label the diagram using descriptive terms.
3. Label the container. Carefully bury your dinosaur shape in the sand.
4. Hold the container of sand over the dishpan and then slowly empty the container of water into the sand. The water will collect in the dishpan.
5. Set the container of sand aside to dry.
6. Exchange containers with a partner.
7. Now it is time to "dig for a dinosaur." Begin by carefully removing the sand to expose the sugar cube dinosaur.
8. When you find the dinosaur, notice how some sand sticks to the sugar and some of the sugar cubes may be missing. Carefully remove the sugar cubes, noting the relationship of one to the next as you set them on a sheet of paper.
9. Try to reconstruct the dinosaur by building another model with 12 sugar cubes.
10. Draw a picture of the dinosaur that you made.
11. Compare the drawing of the reconstructed dinosaur to the original picture drawn by your partner.

My Dinosaur Model

Reconstructed Dinosaur

Questions: *Answer the questions on the back of the paper.*

1. What were the differences between the original drawing of the dinosaur and the dinosaur that you uncovered?
2. What happened to the sugar cubes to make them look different than when they were originally constructed?
3. What do you think could be the effect of water on actual fossil remains in rock?
4. Why is being a paleontologist like being a detective?

METEOROLOGY

Fascinating Facts for Teachers

The Water Cycle

The planet earth is the only planet where water can be found in all three states—solid, liquid, and gas. A major concept in weather studies is the water cycle. The water cycle is considered a closed cycle because all of the water that is present on earth was here when the earth was formed and will be here when the earth is consumed in the death throes of our dying sun. The water cycle explains the ways that water is used and recycled by the earth system. Human impact upon this cycle is important, for the earth will receive no new water supplies. Thus, understanding the concept of the water cycle can stimulate discussions of pollution and lead to a better understanding of conservation of water resources.

COMPONENTS OF THE WATER CYCLE

See Portal for Exploration "What Goes Up Must Come Down"

Using the diagram, it is easiest to begin with evaporation, the process by which liquid water becomes gaseous and enters the atmosphere from the oceans, lakes, and puddles of the world. The water, now a gas called water vapor, rises in the atmosphere until it is cooled to the point where it returns to the liquid state in the form of tiny droplets held suspended in the air. This process is called condensation, and is responsible for the formation of clouds. Clouds can be moved by wind, and the resulting movement of the water is called transportation. When sufficient water vapor continues to condense, and the water droplets become too large to remain suspended, the droplets fall to the earth's surface as precipitation. The precipitation can become either run-off by moving along the surface in streams, or seepage should the water soak into the soil and rock. Some of the water found in soil and rock (called ground water) is used by plants in their life processes and is given back to the atmosphere by the plants in a process called transpiration.

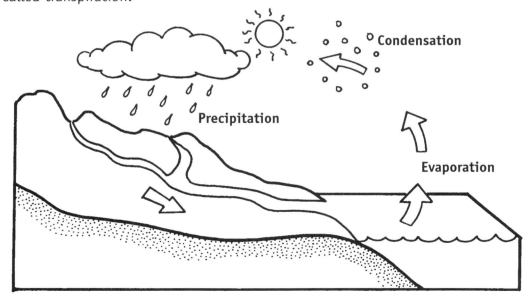

HUMIDITY

When water is present in the atmosphere as water vapor, it is called humidity. Humidity is usually measured in a ratio of the amount of water that is actually in the air, compared to the amount of water that the air could hold. This maximum amount varies according to the temperature and pressure of the air. Thus, it is more meaningful to know the percentage that describes how close the water content is to its maximum than it is to know the actual amount of water that is in an air sample. The actual amount of water in air is called absolute humidity and is generally not used. The ratio of water actually in air compared to the maximum amount of water that the air could hold at a given temperature is called relative humidity, and it is part of most weather reports. When air reaches one hundred percent relative humidity, the air is said to be saturated, or holding the maximum amount of water that it can possibly hold. Should any additional water enter that air, condensation will occur. Often, cold ground will cause warm, moist air to leave a coating of water on the colder grass and dirt as dew. A cold glass of water or a cold window pane, will cause dew to form on the side toward the warmer, moist air. Thus, the temperature at which one hundred percent humidity is reached is called the dew point.

If the air is holding a lot of water compared to the amount that it holds at maximum, the air is said to have a high humidity. High humidity air causes a number of problems in the life of human beings. Some individuals with difficulties in breathing find their physical problems increase in high humidity. High humidity also tends to be present in areas with a great amount of plant life, and thus, a high level of pollen. Many people sensitive to high humidity have moved, for the benefit of their health, to desert areas that have much lower humidities. Many less important effects can also be seen in areas with high humidity. Wooden structures are more difficult to protect in high humidity conditions, and hair actually stretches in high humidity conditions, making the hair more difficult to style. Hair can be used, in fact, as a component of a device that measures humidity. This device is called a hair hygrometer.

See Portal for Exploration "Hair Hygrometer"

CLOUDS

As water vapor is lifted to higher altitudes in the atmosphere, the air and water vapor are cooled. As air is cooled, the maximum amount of water vapor that the air can hold is reduced. As a result, air that is rising also has a rising relative humidity, since the conditions that describe relative humidity are changing. Should the air rise to an altitude that causes the relative humidity to reach one-hundred percent, or the dew point, the water vapor will begin to condense into tiny water droplets around particles of dust. These tiny water droplets are held suspended by the atmosphere and, when in sufficient numbers, can be seen as clouds. It is important to remember that cloud formation requires sufficient water vapor, and some kind of condensation nuclei such as dust, sand, or other particles.

See Portal for Exploration "How Clouds Are Formed"

The shape of the cloud is determined by conditions in the atmosphere in which the cloud is formed, and can be an indicator of what kind of weather will happen in the future. The bottom of all clouds is flat, since the cloud forms at a specific altitude when rising air reaches its dew point. The tops of clouds, however, can appear differently. There are three basic types of clouds: cumulus, stratus, and cirrus. Small puffy clouds that look like cotton balls and are scattered around the sky are called cumulus, and are an indicator of good weather. Other prefixes and suffixes can be added to the term cumulus to give it special meaning. Very tall, puffy clouds are called towering cumulus, and can develop further into the extremely large and violent cumulonimbus, or thunderstorms. The term "nimbus" means rain, and may not always be violent. Flat layered clouds are called stratus, and nimbostratus clouds can produce a steady gentle rain. Middle altitude clouds are given a prefix of "alto" and can be puffy altocumulus or flat altostratus. Very high, wispy clouds are called cirrus and can indicate an approaching change in weather conditions; because they form at such high altitudes, they are made up of ice crystals. These crystals are capable of bending light from the moon, sometimes making it appear as if the moon has a halo.

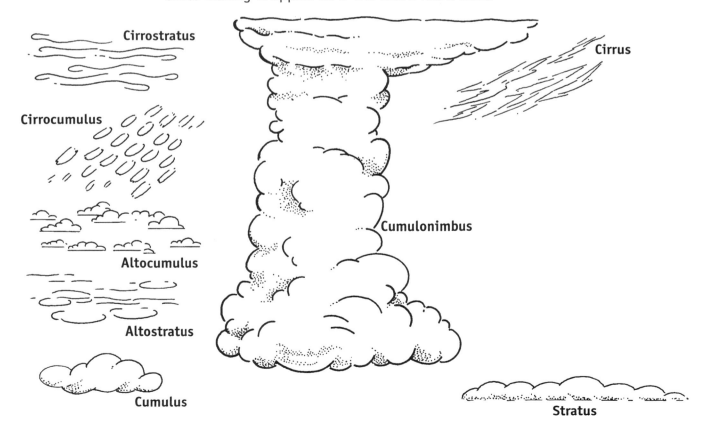

Cirrostratus

Cirrus

Cirrocumulus

Altocumulus

Cumulonimbus

Altostratus

Cumulus

Stratus

Weather

AIR MASSES

One interesting characteristic of air is that air that has different conditions of temperature and humidity does not mix well. As a result, air forms large units, called air masses, that have the conditions of the region over which the air mass forms. What we recognize as weather is actually the conditions of the air mass in which we find ourselves, and the conditions that are brought about by the transition as one air mass moves and is replaced by another. The border between air masses is called a front, and weather conditions at a front are determined by the characteristics of the air mass leaving an area, and the air mass replacing it.

Air masses can form over continents (continental) or over the oceans (maritime), they can be colder or warmer than the land over which they travel, and they can form in areas that tend to be warm (tropical) or cold (polar). Air masses are named in a three character sequence on the basis of these characteristics. The first lowercase letter defines where the air mass formed: "m" for maritime or "c" for continental. The middle, uppercase letter describes if the air mass formed over a warm tropical area ("T") or a cold polar area ("P"). The third character tells whether the air mass is colder than the land over which it is travelling ("k") or warmer ("w"). A moist air mass formed over a warm body of water (like the Gulf of Mexico) that is warmer than the land over which it is traveling would be named "mTw". A dry air mass, colder than the land over which it travels, that was formed over the northern reaches of Canada would be labeled as "cPk".

FRONTS

Fronts are the borders between air masses. As one air mass moves to be replaced by another, the border passes bringing with it a distinctive weather pattern determined by the nature of the two air masses involved. If the replacement air mass is colder that the first, the boundary, named for the replacement air, is called a cold front. If the air mass moving into an area is warmer than what was there previously, then the front is called a warm front. If the air masses should become stalled and stop moving, then the front also stops moving. This condition is called a stationary front.

Cold fronts, named for the cold air mass replacing a warmer air mass, take on characteristics determined by the way the cold air moves into an area. Cold air is more dense and moves along the surface of the earth throwing the warm air before it high into the air. Its movement is reminiscent of a fast moving bulldozer. The weather associated with this kind of front usually brings "violent" weather conditions, including thunderstorms, as the colder air moves into an area.

See Portal for Exploration "Warm and Cold Front Movement"

Warm fronts signal that warm air, less dense than the air it is replacing, is entering an area. The less dense warm air is not very effective at pushing the denser cold air out of its way. The warmer air tends to slip over the top of the cold air along a very gentle, inclined, frontal boundary. This boundary can extend for hundreds of miles in advance of the warmer air and tends to bring with it a slow moving and gentle period of rain.

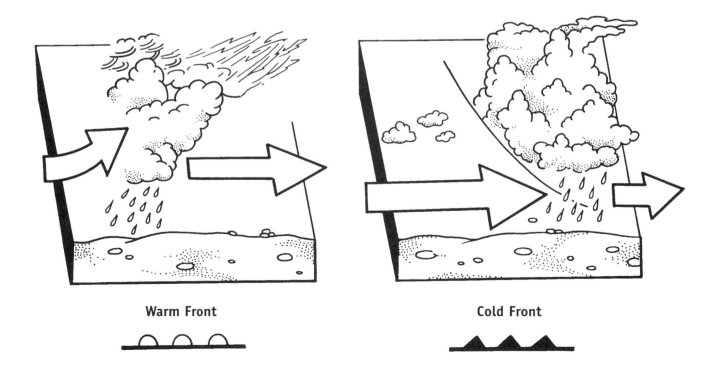

Warm Front

Cold Front

A stationary front brings weather that has the characteristics of the front it was originally before stopping, continuing for a longer period of time until it begins to move again. An occluded front marks where a cold front actually overtakes a warm front, lifting the entire warm front into the air. It is in this type of front that extreme weather is most often seen, since the entire warm air mass is lifted upward by the more dense cold air mass. The gentle conditions of a warm front are followed by severe weather in this type of front.

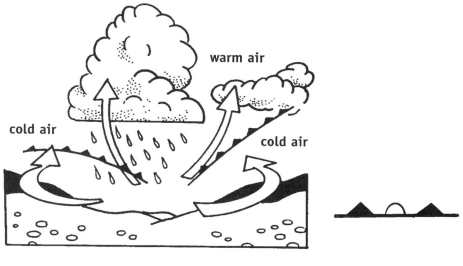

Occluded Front

OBSERVATIONS

See Portal for Exploration "Weather Tracking and Forecasting"
Several aspects of weather are routinely measured and widely reported. The temperature is usually reported in degrees Fahrenheit/Celsius. These measurements are made with a thermometer. Many families have outdoor thermometers attached to their homes in order to determine what is appropriate wear for the out-of-doors.

Atmospheric pressure is another common weather measurement. The measurement is made using an instrument called the barometer. The reading is usually reported in terms of the height in inches of a column of mercury (in. Hg) that can be supported by the pressure exerted by the atmosphere. The most accurate barometers still use a glass column of mercury open to the atmosphere only at its lower end. Recent cautions on the poisonous effects of mercury have made the aneroid barometer more common and easier to use. It uses a totally empty can (aneroid means without air) and indicates, by means of a needle, the amount that the can is crushed or is expanded as atmospheric pressure increases or decreases, respectively. Low pressure occurs where air is rising, and usually signals bad weather conditions. Higher pressure occurs where air is descending and usually signals good weather. As a barometer's reading moves toward low pressure or toward high pressure, appropriate changes toward bad or good weather, respectively, can be expected.

Precipitation is measured by the use of a rain gauge. It is a container that catches the rain and funnels it into a graduated, or marked, cylinder. The graduations indicate the number of inches/centimeters of rainfall that has been captured by the funnel.

Wind is also measured and reported. Wind direction uses a type of weather vane and is reported as a direction of the compass. Wind is named for the direction from which it blows. Wind that comes from the north is a north wind, or northerly, just as wind that comes from the south is southernly. The wind speed is measured by an anemometer, a device that the wind spins. The faster the wind blows, the more rapid is the rotation of the anemometer.

Cloud type and the amount of sky covered by clouds is also routinely reported. The observer may use a reference key when identifying the cloud type if the clouds are not easily recognized. The coverage is usually reported in tenths of the sky: ten tenths coverage is overcast, 5 tenths is partly cloudy, and 0 tenths is clear.

WEATHER PHENOMENON

See Portal for Exploration "Layers of the Atmosphere"

The atmosphere can be divided into layers as determined by temperature changes that occur within each layer. The troposphere, the lowest layer of the atmosphere and extending less that 35 kilometers from the surface of the earth, is a layer in which the temperature decreases as altitude increases. When the temperature stops decreasing, the top of the troposphere is nearing. The layers are not a fixed thickness, but they change over time in response to many variables. Most weather phenomena occur in this lowest layer.

The most common of the violent weather phenomenon are thunderstorms. Most feared for its ability to produce striking lightening and high winds, the thunderstorm is a result of the mature development of the cumulonimbus cloud. Updrafts within the clouds are very strong and are credited with playing a part in the generation of static electricity charges. When the positive static electricity charges near the bottom of a cumulonimbus cloud accumulate to a sufficient amount, the charge "grounds" with the delivery of electrons from either the top of the same cloud, a different cloud, or from the ground. The lightening that is dangerous to us actually travels in an interesting way. While "tracer lightening" fingers down to the ground from the cloud, the main bolt actually travels up from the ground using the path of least resistance as found by the tracer lightening. In the event of a thunderstorm, a person should seek the protection of a structure. If caught in an open field, you should lie down in an effort to allow surroundings to become "taller" and, thus, more likely to attract lightening away from you.

See Portal for Exploration "Tornado in a Bottle"

In some very large thunderstorms called supercells, in processes not fully understood, rotation of the entire cloud can give rise to small, extremely violent, whirling phenomenon called tornadoes. Tornadoes occur in many countries, but are more common in the United States. They strike every state but are more often found in an area of the Midwest between the Rocky Mountains and the Mississippi River called "Tornado Alley." The highest wind speeds ever measured are generated in the vortex of a tornado. Meteorologists, with special types of radar, have become more able to predict where tornado activity will occur, but the tornado's path of destruction can be complete and its direction unpredictable. In the event that you are caught in weather that is associated with a tornado, finding shelter is critical. The best shelter is in a basement or the interior of very strong building.

A very large low pressure weather system is called a hurricane. Hurricanes develop in the warmer waters of the Atlantic Ocean near the equator, typically, during the months of June, July, and August. They may measure hundreds of miles across and they generate cloud formations that can impact weather observations for a thousand miles/kilometers. Hurricanes are the largest storms on earth generating wind speeds of at least 74 miles (119 km) per hour. The damage caused by hurricanes includes wind damage, damage from associated thunderstorms and tornadoes, and water damage from extreme amounts of rain and a rise in sea level in the vicinity of the hurricane. These storms are very large, and evacuations, when required, are widely announced by the media.

Climate and Seasons

EARTH POSITION

The earth moves through space in four ways. It is traveling through the galaxy with the rest of the solar system, it revolves around the sun once each year, it rotates on its axis, and the axis "wobbles" as it moves like a gyroscope in a motion called gyroscopic procession. Since the gyroscopic procession takes thousands of years to complete a wobble, it does not figure into weather very much. And since the entire solar system is moving through the galaxy, that also does not affect weather significantly. However, the revolution of the earth around the sun and the rotation of the earth on its axis do affect weather.

See Portal for
Exploration
"The Coriolis Effect"

The sun is the source of the energy that powers the atmosphere as the earth rotates like a meal being rotated on a spit over a fire. Solar radiation crosses the vacuum of space and heats the atmosphere unevenly depending on the latitude, the amount of radiation that is absorbed by the atmosphere, and the earth's surface under it. The atmosphere around the equator, for instance, receives much more radiation than the atmosphere near the poles of the earth. Therefore, the air around the equator tend to rise, having been heated and becoming less dense. The air at the poles receives less heat, becomes more dense, and tends to sink toward the surface of the earth. Air, given a motionless earth, then, would flow from the equator to the poles. Since the earth does rotate, a phenomenon called the Coriolis effect gives this wind a "twist" as viewed from the earth, and major wind belts are formed.

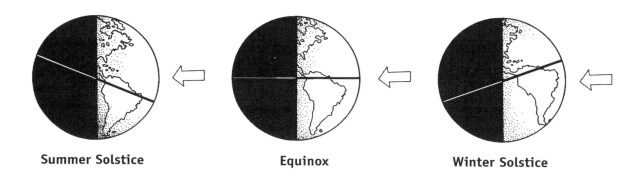

Summer Solstice   **Equinox**   **Winter Solstice**

SEASONS

See Portal for
Exploration
"What Causes the
Seasons?"

The axis is not perpendicular to the plane of orbit; it is inclined at 23.5 degrees. Due to this inclination, the Northern and Southern Hemispheres are not heated evenly as the earth revolves around the sun. At one point in a revolution, or a year, the Northern Hemisphere is inclined toward the sun and intercepts more of the sun's radiation than the Southern Hemisphere. The point at which this inclination is the greatest is the Northern Hemisphere's summer solstice (and the Southern Hemisphere's winter), June 21-22. The opposite situation occurs during the Northern Hemisphere's winter solstice, December 21. At this point, the Northern Hemisphere is tilted away from the sun. At the points in the earth's revolution between the solstices, the earth is inclined, still toward the star Polaris, but in a way that each hemisphere receives the same solar radiation. For two days each year, the daytime and nighttime hours are the same: twelve hours. The days of the "equal night" are called the autumnal equinox (Sept 21-22) and vernal equinox (March 22-23), the first days of fall and spring, respectively.

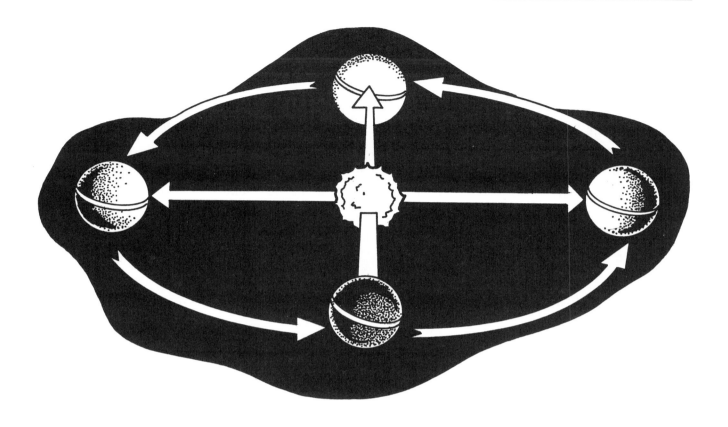

Earth Revolving Around the Sun

CLIMATE

The climate of an area is the average weather over an extended period of time. Conditions such as temperature, rainfall, humidity, wind direction, and seasonal changes tend to remain the same or go through similar annual changes in any area. A number of factors can influence climate including location on the earth, especially near mountain ranges; the amount of sunlight reaching the earth; relationship between land and water; and altitude. Generally, the climate of an area remains, on average, the same for very long periods of time. It is important that students recognize that their actions can accelerate changes in the climate. Humans can create changes in climate locally, such as the effect that cities have on their immediate areas, or globally, by affecting the ability of the atmosphere to radiate excess heat off into space. The latter is caused by the accumulation of gasses (like carbon dioxide) in the atmosphere resulting from pollution from industries, automobiles, and much more.

Portals for Learning: Literature

Aardema, V. *Bringing the Rain to Kapiti Plain*. Dial Books, 1981.
A fictitious story about a drought's effect on an African plain and the herds of cows that graze there, as well as the herdsmen's attempts to start the rain.

Barrett, J. *Cloudy with a Chance of Meatballs*. Scholastic, 1978.
This fictional tale involves a characteristic of weather, constant change. As different food falls from the sky as precipitation, children can learn of weather changes.

Berger, M. & Berger, G. *How's the Weather?* Ideals Children's Books, 1993.
The factual book offers the reader simple explanations of how and why the weather is always different and the difficulties encountered with forecasting the weather.

Branley, F. M. *Hurricane Watch*. Harper, 1985.
Offers the reader information on events associated with a hurricane, characteristics of hurricanes, and what to do in an emergency.

Caduto, M. J. & Bruchac, J. *Keepers of the Earth*. Fulcrum, 1989.
A collection of Native American legend and lore accompanied by activities that address the topics contained in the legends

Carlstron, N.W. *What Does the Rain Play?* Macmillan, 1993.
An aesthetic approach to the sounds and rhythm of a rainstorm

Chapman, C. *Snow on Snow on Snow*. Scholastic, 1994.
This fictional tale features a little boy looking for his dog which is lost in the snow. It discusses activities to do in the snow such as sleigh riding.

Cole, J. *The Magic School Bus: At the Waterworks*. Scholastic, 1986.
A fictional account of Ms. Frizzle and her class as they take a wild trip through the water cycle

Cole, J. *The Magic School Bus: Inside a Hurricane*. Scholastic, 1995.
This is a fictional account of Ms. Frizzle and her class as they explore the structure and stages of a hurricane. Packed with facts, this book offers the reader a detailed description of the phenomena.

Cole, S. *When the Rain Stops*. Lothrop, Lee & Shepard, 1991.
A little girl is chased home as a storm approaches but finds out that there is rain inside as well as outside (due to a leaky roof). When the rain stops, she and her father experience a changed outdoors. The book briefly describes the journey of the water cycle once it reaches the ground.

Coleridge, S. *January Brings the Snow*. Simon & Schuster, 1987.
Describes the changes that occur each month as the year progresses through the seasons.

DePaola, T. *The Cloud Book*. Holiday House, 1975.
This book offers a detailed description of how clouds are classified and named. Additionally, it provides the reader with background on weather folklore.

Dewey, A. *The Sky*. Green Tiger Press, 1993.
Points out to the reader all of the wonderful surprises the sky holds if you take time to look at it. Uses a very creative approach to weaving text throughout the pictures.

Dorrs, A. *Me and My Shadow*. Scholastic, 1990.
This book helps the reader investigate shadows. It also discusses the positions of the sun and moon and their relationship to shadows.

Ganeri, A. *And Now the Weather*. Aladdin, 1992.
A factual book that describes what causes the seasons, how winds form, and the water cycle's role in the weather

Gibbons, G. *Weather Forecasting*. Simon & Schuster, 1987.
The author takes the reader on a behind the scenes trip to a weather station as she examines the instruments used by meteorologists in the process of making a weather forecast.

Jeffers, S. *Brother Eagle, Sister Sky*. Scholastic, 1991.
This book presents a message (albeit disputed) from Chief Seattle on the value of the environment, including the atmosphere. It echoes the close relationship between nature and the Native American cultures.

Jeunesse, G. & Valat, P-M. *Water*. Cartwheel Books, 1990.
A factual book about water on the earth, it uses acetate overlays to help explain concepts to children.

Kandolan, E. *Molly's Seasons*. Cobblehill Books, 1992.
A wonderful book in which Molly journeys through the four seasons, identifying important dates and positions of the earth and sun. Also briefly discusses seasons at the equator and poles.

Keats, E. J. *The Snowy Day*. Scholastic, 1962.
Describes a young boy's adventures as he investigates a snowfall.

Peters, L. W. *The Sun, the Wind, and the Rain*. Henry Holt, 1988.
Discusses the weather's role in shaping the earth and helping erode land, as it compares the long geologic cycle to a little girl's sand mountain.

Pfister, M. *Hopper*. Scholastic, 1991.
Describes the adventures of a snow hare and his mother as they search for food in the winter and the obstacles they need to overcome.

Polacco, P. *Thunder Cake*. Philomel, 1990.
A fictional tale of how a grandmother helps her granddaughter overcome her fear of thunder and lightening by focusing her attention on baking a cake

Serfozo, M. *Rain Talk*. Scholastic, 1990.
This is a whimsical tale of a little girl's experience of a rainstorm. She describes the sound the rain makes as it falls softly and then begins to intensify.

Simon, S. *Storms*. Morrow, 1987.
An excellent book that identifies atmospheric conditions during severe weather storms. Actual photographs are included.

Stinson, K. *Red is Best*. Annick Press LTD, 1982.
A story that describes a young child's choices about how to dress for school based on what she likes rather than what she needs

Tomkins, J. *Nimby, an Extraordinary Cloud Who Meets a Remarkable Friend*. Green Tiger Press, 1982.
A fictional tale of a cloud who encounters an island and its effects on the cloud

What Goes Up Must Come Down

Purpose:
- Model the water cycle within a terrarium.
- Identify and define components of the water cycle as modeled in the terrarium.

Materials Needed:
aluminum foil
potting soil
water
activated charcoal

fish tank gravel or small pebbles
various house plants
scissors

Classroom project:
large aquarium
Plexiglass covering
silicone sealer

Student project:
2-liter soda bottle

Procedure: **Student Project**
See instructions on student lab sheet.

Classroom Project
1. Cut a piece of Plexiglass to fit on the top of the aquarium.
2. In the aquarium, put a layer of aluminum foil, a 25 mm layer of gravel, a 25 mm layer of charcoal, and then 7 to 10 cm of potting soil.
3. Plant small plants in the soil, then water moderately to moisten the soil.
4. Place the piece of Plexiglass on top of the aquarium and seal with a silicone sealer (can be purchased in a hardware store). It now becomes the top of the terrarium and the seal prevents moisture from escaping.
5. Place the terrarium in a sunny part of the room.

Behind the Scenes: With a little luck your terrarium and water cycle will be self-sufficient. Students can observe water droplets forming on the top of the terrarium (condensation). Sometimes on a hot day it will look cloudy or steamy in the terrarium which indicates that evaporation is occurring and although a steady rain will not fall, students can observe water droplets falling back to the soil (precipitation).

Answer Key For Questions:
1. Condensation
2. Some of the moisture in the soil evaporates into the air. The moist air near the top surface of the terrarium cools, causing water droplets to collect on the surface. These water droplets run down the inside surface of the bottle and moisten the soil.

Literature Links:
Cole, J. *The Magic School Bus: At the Waterworks.* Scholastic, 1986.
Cole, S. *When the Rain Stops.* Lothrop, Lee & Shepard, 1991.
DePaola, T. *The Cloud Book.* Holiday House, 1975.
Ganeri, A. *And Now the Weather.* Aladdin, 1992.
Jeunesse, G. & Valat, P-M. *Water.* Cartwheel Books, 1990.
Tomkins, J. *Nimby, an Extraordinary Cloud Who Meets a Remarkable Friend.* Green Tiger Press, 1982.

Portals for Expansion:

Language Arts
- Create a journal and record the daily changes observed with the terrariums and water cycles.
- Write haiku poetry about the process that occurs in the water cycle.
- Write letters regarding the state of the local environment to local government, companies in environmental business, and companies that seem to be impacting negatively on the environment. Letters can also be written to weather forecasting stations to request copies of weather maps and/or tours.

Science
- Research and build a rain gauge. Using this weather instrument, record the amount of rainfall for a duration of time.
- Study global weather patterns. Share your observations with other students.
- Create a mud puddle somewhere on school property and have the students make observations of what happens over time.

Social Studies
- Read *Bringing the Rain to Kapiti Plain* by V. Aardema and have the students discuss why some areas do not have as much rainfall or seasonal rains as others.

Art and Music
- Create a wall size mural on butcher paper of the water cycle making sure the students include land features of their local area as well as the parts of the water cycle.

Math
- Calculate, using fractions or decimals, how much of the earth's water is freshwater, saltwater, and locked in glaciers.

What Goes Up Must Come Down

Procedure:

1. Cut off the top of the bottle with a pair of scissors so that the top of the bottle is separate from the bottom.

2. Pull off the hard plastic bottom of the bottle. You may have to soak the bottle in warm water to loosen the glue.

3. Inside the hard plastic bottom, begin with a layer of aluminum, add a layer of gravel, a layer of charcoal, and then potting soil.

4. Make a small hole in the potting soil.

5. Set the plant in the hole and then fill the hole with soil. Water the plant.

6. Place the top part of the bottle over the black bottom so it acts like a dome over the plant.

7. Place the terrarium in a sunny part of the room.

Questions:

1. What forms on the inside of the dome of the terrarium?

2. Describe how the terrarium models the water cycle that occurs on earth.

The Hair Hygrometer

Purpose:
- Observe the effect of humidity on hair by constructing a device that measures changing length of hair.
- Correlate the indicated changes of length of hair to the relative humidity of the air.

Materials Needed:

piece of cleaned long hair (e.g., horse hair)   milk carton
bamboo skewer   white glue
76 x 127 mm card   oak tag
fine felt-tip marker

Procedure: See instructions on student lab sheet.

Answer Key For Questions:
1. Answers will vary. For example, the hair will lengthen or relax.
2. Answers will vary. For example, the hair will shrink or become shorter.
3. Answers will vary. For example, the hair arrangement is difficult to manage.

Literature Links:
Berger, M., & Berger, G. *How's the Weather?* Ideals Children's Books, 1993.
Ganeri, A. *And Now the Weather.* Aladdin, 1992.
Gibbons, G. *Weather Forecasting.* Simon & Schuster, 1987.
Jeunesse, G., & Valat, P-M. *Water.* Cartwheel Books, 1990.

Portals for Expansion:

Language Arts
- Write a report on the water cycle and how water vapor enters the air.

Science
- Interview an airplane pilot to find out the effect of humidity on the performance of airplanes flying through the air.

Social Studies
- Research the geographic influences on the humidity of a particular region including bodies of water and locations of mountains.

Health and Safety
- Invite a guest speaker to speak on the topic of health problems that may be related to conditions of humidity.

Math
- Create a graph that records the humidity levels in your region.
- Estimate readings on the hair hygrometer that have not actually been observed using the math process skill of extrapolation.

The Hair Hygrometer

Procedure:
1. Cut off the bottom of the milk carton, opposite the sealed flap.
2. Put a small hole in the top of the carton in the center near the sealed flap.
3. Cut an indicator arrow from oak tag.
4. Draw an arc on a 76 x 127 mm card.
5. Glue the card onto the carton with the arc center being the skewer and the rest of the card extending toward the sealed flap of the carton.
6. Carefully push the pointer onto the skewer and secure with a drop of white glue.
7. Careful push one end of a horse hair though the hole in the top of the carton and tie a large knot in the end of the horse hair so that it does not slip through the hole in the top.
8. Tie the other end around the skewer.
9. Secure the horse hair at both ends using a drop of white glue.
10. When the glue is dry, rotate the pointer until the horse hair is tight and the pointer indicates a spot on the card. Mark this spot on the card and then record what this value is after checking a weather report. You now have a working hygrometer.
11. During the next few weeks, continue this experiment until 12 different readings are recorded on the card and the values they represent.

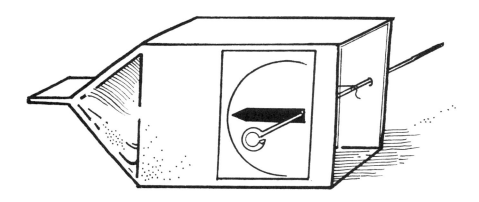

Questions:
1. What happens to the hair when conditions are very humid?

2. What happens to the hair when conditions are very dry?

3. How does this apply to people who say they are having a "bad hair day?"

How Clouds Are Formed

Purpose:
- List the components necessary for cloud formation.
- Use the needed components to model cloud formation.
- Apply knowledge of the components for cloud formation to answer questions regarding clouds in our environment.

Materials Needed:
clear plastic bottle with cap
incense to use as smoke source
water

Procedure:
See instructions on student lab sheet.

Answer Key For Questions:
1. No
2. Answers will vary. For example, smoke or condensation nuclei is also necessary.
3. Answers will vary. For example, on the windward side of the mountains, air is made to rise.
4. Answers will vary. For example, if sufficient humidity is present, the smoke would serve as condensation nuclei.

Literature Links:
Berger, M., & Berger, G. *How's the Weather?* Ideals Children's Books, 1993.
DePaola, T. *The Cloud Book.* Holiday House, 1975.
Dewey, A. *The Sky.* Green Tiger Press, 1993.
Ganeri, A. *And Now the Weather.* Aladdin, 1992.
Gibbons, G. *Weather Forecasting.* Simon & Schuster, 1987.
Jeunesse, G. & Valat, P-M. *Water.* Cartwheel Books, 1990.
Tomkins, J. *Nimby, an Extraordinary Cloud Who Meets a Remarkable Friend.* Green Tiger Press, 1982.

Portals for Expansion:

Language Arts
- Write stories about pictures students see in the clouds using narrative descriptive essays.

Art
- Create drawings, picture, murals, or 3-D dioramas portraying the images students see in cloud formations.
- Identify the variety of blue hues using paint sample cards from the hardware or paint store.

Social Studies
- Research the effect of geography on the development of clouds, including such terms as land breeze, sea breeze, windward, and leeward.
- Research the effect of human activity on the development of clouds (e.g., acid rain, cloud seeding, and effects of cooling towers).

How Clouds Are Formed

Procedure:
1. Place 50 mL of water inside a plastic bottle.
2. Shake the bottle, then squeeze it hard for 15 seconds, then suddenly stop squeezing.
3. Describe the interior of the bottle.

4. Uncap the bottle. While squeezing the bottle place the mouth of the bottle near the burning incense. Stop squeezing so that some of the smoke enters the bottle. Recap the bottle.

5. Shake the bottle, squeeze it for 15 seconds, and then stop squeezing.
6. Describe the interior of the bottle with low pressure.

7. Now squeeze the bottle tightly and hold for 15 seconds.
8. Describe the interior of the bottle under pressure.

Questions: *Answer the questions on the back of the paper.*
1. Do water and pressure changes alone cause clouds to form?
2. What is necessary, in addition to water and pressure changes, to form a cloud?
3. Pressure changes can be caused by changes in altitude. What function does a mountain range serve in the formation of clouds?
4. Why do some farmers believe that putting smoke into the air can cause the formation of clouds?

Warm and Cold Front Movement

Purpose:
- Investigate the effect of temperature on the relative densities of a fluid.
- Apply this knowledge in the construction of a model of two types of weather fronts.
- Define the terms cold front and warm front.
- Explain the differences between the characteristics of cold and warm fronts.

Materials Needed:

plastic shoe box	2-250 mL beakers	red and blue food coloring
long neck funnel	wood block	tongs
water	ice	thermometer
dishpan	hot plate	

Procedure:
1. *Note:* This investigation can be used as a teacher demonstration or completed by older responsible students with adult supervision. It is important to allow the water to become room temperature.
2. See instructions on student lab sheet.

Answer Key For Questions:
1. Blue. Answers will vary. For example, it sinks to the bottom of the container.
2. Red. Answers will vary. For example, it floats on top of the room temperature water.
3. Blue water
4. Red water
5. Blue water
6. Cold air
7. Cold fronts
8. Answers will vary. For example, in cold fronts, cold air is more dense and moves more quickly thus creating a greater rate of change.

Literature Links:
Aardema, V. *Bringing the Rain to Kapiti Plain*. Dial, 1981.
Barrett, J. *Cloudy with a Chance of Meatballs*. Scholastic, 1978.
Berger, M. & Berger, G. *How's the Weather?* Ideals Children's Books, 1993.
Ganeri, A. *And Now the Weather*. Aladdin, 1992.
Gibbons, G. *Weather Forecasting*. Simon & Schuster, 1987.

Portals for Expansion:

Language Arts
- Write to pen pals in order to exchange information about how weather changes affects daily life.
- Write about the kinds of activities students do on rainy days, or about events that happened during storms in their communities.

Math
- Calculate how fast fronts move by checking newspaper reports of weather and measuring distances involved in the flow of weather across the nation.

Social Studies
- Conduct library research on the effect of geographical features that affect weather patterns (e.g., mountain ranges).

Warm and Cold Front Movement

Procedure: Assemble the plastic shoe box and wood block as shown in the diagram. Fill the plastic shoe box about one-quarter full of water.

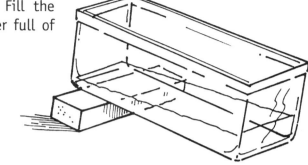

1. Record the temperature of the water:

    _____°C

2. Prepare the two beakers:
    • Pour about 175 mL of water into each beaker.
    • Put several drops of red food coloring into one beaker.
    • Add several drops of blue in the other beaker.

3. Place the red water beaker on a hot plate. Place the blue water beaker into the container of ice.

4. Allow the temperature of the cold water to fall about 15 degrees.

    • Record the final temperature: _____°C

5. Pour the cold water into a long neck funnel that extends to the bottom of the shallow end of the plastic shoe box.

6. Describe how the cold water moves:

7. Allow the temperature of the warm water to rise about 15 degrees.

    • Record the final temperature: _____°C

8. Using tongs to avoid touching the hot beaker, gently pour the warm water into the long neck funnel placed at the shallow end of the plastic shoe box.

9. Describe how the warm water moves:

Questions:

1. Which colored water is more dense than the room temperature water? How do you know?

2. Which colored water is less dense than the room temperature water? How do you know?

3. Cold fronts are named for the cold air that replaces warmer air. Is the red water or the blue water demonstration more like a cold front?

4. Warm fronts are named for the warm air that replaces cooler air. Is the red water or the blue water demonstration more like warm air trying to push cold air out of the way?

5. Was the blue water or red water in contact with the bottom of the container more quickly?

6. If the water is like air, and the bottom of the container is like the earth's surface, which kind of air, warm or cold, affects the surface of the earth more quickly?

7. Would cold fronts or warm fronts affect the weather more quickly?

8. Can you explain the differences between a cold front and a warm front in terms of density and rate of weather changes?

Weather Tracking and Forecasting

Purpose:
- Track the weather in the local area by keeping records of weather data on the Weather Tracking Data Sheet.
- Compose and record in the data sheet a 24-hour forecast based on the students' earlier recorded observations.

Materials Needed:

weather maps from newspapers	symbols for weather tracking
barometer	thermometer
rain gauge	anemometer
wind sock or compass	crayons or markers
glue	scissors
construction paper	

Procedure:
1. Review weather maps from the newspaper with the students. Have the students observe how each type of observation is recorded.
2. Reproduce the Weather Tracking Data Sheet for each student. You may prefer to enlarge the data sheet before making multiple copies.
3. Students should begin tracking the weather on a Monday by recording temperature, wind direction, wind speed, cloud type, sky cover, rainfall, barometric pressure, and trend.
4. Students should look for a day when the weather conditions were similar based on one or several of the pieces of data being recorded.
5. Students should make a forecast for the following day based on the conditions that follow the data they have identified as being similar.
6. Check the forecast the next day for accuracy.

Literature Links:
Barrett, J. *Cloudy with a Chance of Meatballs*. Scholastic, 1978.
Berger, M., & Berger, G. *How's the Weather?* Ideals Children's Books, 1993.
Branley, F. M. *Hurricane Watch*. Harper Trophy Books, 1985.
Cole, J. *The Magic School Bus: Inside a Hurricane*. Scholastic, 1995.
DePaola, T. *The Cloud Book*. Holiday House, 1975.
Ganeri, A. *And Now the Weather*. Aladdin, 1992.
Gibbons, G. *Weather Forecasting*. Simon & Schuster, 1987.
Simon, S. *Storms*. Morrow, 1987.

Portals for Expansion:

Language Arts
- Have students prepare weather reports based on their observations at their school site. These weather reports can become part of the daily school announcements.
- Prepare a weather journal that deals with issues of weather, a person's health and feelings, and so on.
- Investigate weather folklore and prepare reports as to the accuracy of the story and tales.
- Read poetry that has a weather theme.

Science
- Conduct an experiment on a sunny day to determine if water or soil heats up quicker. Place a thermometer in a bowl of water and a second one in a bowl of soil. Place both in a sunny location and record the temperature after an hour.
- Encourage students to investigate what role conduction, convection, and radiation have in weather systems.

Social Studies
- Relate geographical locations and the types of severe weather that are experienced at that location.
- Use the points of the compass in reporting weather observations or practice telling directions using both compasses and maps.

Math
- Create charts and graphs of the weather observations made by students. Temperature averages, total rainfall, etc. are all part of normal weather reporting systems.

Art and Music
- Play games that recreate the rhythms of rain and rainstorms. They can also simulate the sounds of storms.
- Explore patterns and shapes of clouds or snowflakes. Students may create three-dimensional models of clouds with cotton or create drawings of a variety of cloud conditions.
- Watch the clouds and construct objects that the clouds resembled.

Warm Front   **Cold Front**

Name

Weather Tracking and Forecasting

Procedure: Record the following information on the Weather Tracking Data Sheet.

1. Record the average temperature (or temperature indicated on your instruments) in the first column of the data sheet.

2. Record the wind direction (using the major compass directions) and speed (in knots) in the next two columns.

3. Record the cloud type by looking at the clouds that you observe in the sky or those recorded in the weather report.

4. Record sky cover in "tenths of the sky" based either on your observations or on the weather report read by your teacher.

5. Record the number of inches or centimeters of rainfall given by either your instruments or in the weather report.

6. Record the air pressure (in inches or centimeters of mercury) given by either your instruments or in the weather report.

7. Record the barometer trend, using one of the following letters:
   • "R" for rising
   • "F" for falling
   • "S" for steady

8. Find a day where the weather conditions were similar. Speculate on what the next day will bring based on the conditions that followed that similar day. Write out your forecast in the next to last column.

9. Check whether the forecast was accurate, then fill in the last space on the chart.

LAB
Geology

Weather Tracking Data Sheet

	Air Temp.	Wind Direction	Wind Speed	Cloud Type	Sky Cover %	Amount of Rainfall	Barometric Pressure	Trend Direction	Forecast for Next Day	Accuracy
Monday date:										
Tuesday date:										
Wednesday date:										
Thursday date:										
Friday date:										
Saturday date:										
Sunday date:										
Monday date:										
Tuesday date:										
Wednesday date:										
Thursday date:										
Friday date:										
Saturday date:										
Sunday date:										

Interactive Bulletin Board
Daily Weather Report

Purpose:
- Maintain a daily weather map that indicates the weather across the United States.
- Predict the weather for the following day in the local area based on the weather patterns.

Materials Needed:

poster board	bulletin board paper
newspaper weather maps	atlas
outline map of your country (page 95)	black marker and removable tape
weather symbols/sheet (page 93-94)	

Procedure:

Setup:
1. Using an overhead projector, enlarge the outline map of your country and trace it onto bulletin board paper. Use a black marker to fill in state/providence boundaries. Laminate this map. Indicate on the edges of the map the Pacific Ocean and Atlantic Ocean.
2. Break students into cooperative learning groups of three to four students. Have each team of students prepare weather map symbols on poster board. Provide newspaper weather maps as a reference. Cut out the symbols and store them in a manila envelope.
3. Make a key to identify the weather symbols for the bulletin board map.
4. Develop a schedule that indicates which team of students is responsible for the weather report each day.

Activity:
1. Introduce the weather map to the students. Discuss how each team of students is responsible for preparing a weather forecast on the assigned day.
2. The report will consist of placing the correct weather symbols (highs, lows, fronts, rain, snow, sleet, sun, etc.) on the map, completing a written daily report that is read to the class, and a forecast for tomorrow's weather.
3. Provide the students with a variety of daily resources (newspapers, access to the Weather Channel, the Internet) that they can use to collect their information for the weather forecast.
4. Allow time each morning for the group to collect their data, develop their weather map, and give the forecast to the class.
5. Set time aside at the end of the day to discuss and evaluate that day's forecast from the previous day.

Behind the Scenes: Weather maps from newspapers will vary. Therefore, it is important to provide a variety of sources from which students can gather their information.

Literature Links:
Barrett, J. *Cloudy with a Chance of Meatballs*. Scholastic, 1978.
Berger, M., & Berger, G. *How's the Weather?* Ideals Children's Books, 1993.
Gibbons, G. *Weather Forecasting*. Simon & Schuster, 1987.

Portals for Expansion:
Math
- Relate with a graph the relationship between temperature and cloud cover.
- Keep a running total and graph of the daily or weekly amount of rainfall using a rain gauge.
Science
- Research ways to construct weather instruments. Build a classroom weather station.

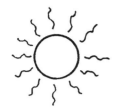 # Daily Weather Report

Date: _____   Time: _____

Weather Report Done By: _____

Current Air Temperature _____

Expected High: _____   Expected Low: _____

Barometric Pressure: _____   Source: _____

Cloud Type: Morning _____

Afternoon _____

Evening _____

Wind Direction: _____

Forecast for Tomorrow:

LAB
Meteorology

LAB
Meteorology

95

Layers of the Atmosphere

Teacher Demonstration

Purpose: • Demonstrate by using liquids with different densities how the layers of the atmosphere do not mix and remain intact.

Materials Needed:
50 mL glycerin (colored blue)
50 mL turpentine (colored red)
50 mL water (colored yellow)
50 mL cooking oil
50 mL alcohol (colored green)
500 mL glass beaker

Procedure:

Setup:
1. Pour the glycerin into the 500 mL beaker.
2. Carefully and slowly pour the turpentine down the side of the beaker making every attempt to prevent it from mixing with the glycerin. The goal is to form a "layer" on top of the glycerin.
3. Repeat Step 2 for the remaining three liquids: the water, then the cooking oil, and finally the alcohol. If you tilt the beaker and slowly pour the liquids down the side, minimal mixing will occur.
4. Allow the beaker to rest for approximately 30 minutes before starting the demonstration.

Demonstration:
1. This demonstration will work well when you are attempting to describe the layers of the atmosphere. Students often cannot understand that air will remain separated.
2. After introducing the concept that there are different layers in the atmosphere, ask the students to illustrate what layers of air would look like. Review vocabulary words, such as layer, (layers in order: troposphere, stratosphere, mesosphere, [ionosphere—lower part of exosphere], and exosphere) and boundary (pauses).
3. Explain to the students that you are going to show them a model of what the layers of the air look like and that you can actually see where two layers meet but do not mix together.
4. Allow the students an opportunity to observe the beaker of liquids closely. Point out the distinct line that occurs between two layers.
5. After all students have had an opportunity to observe the model, provide them with the handout and ask them to label the layers and identify their importance.

Behind the Scenes: If for some reason, the liquids end up mixing together, do not worry! The liquids will eventually separate themselves into layers as long as they have not been shaken vigorously. It will just take longer for this to happen. If students are having difficulty seeing the distinct lines that form, allow natural light to shine on the beaker.

The proper disposal of the liquids is important. Since the mixture contains turpentine, you may not be allowed to dump it down the drain. Please check with your school's custodian for proper disposal procedures.

Layers of the Atmosphere

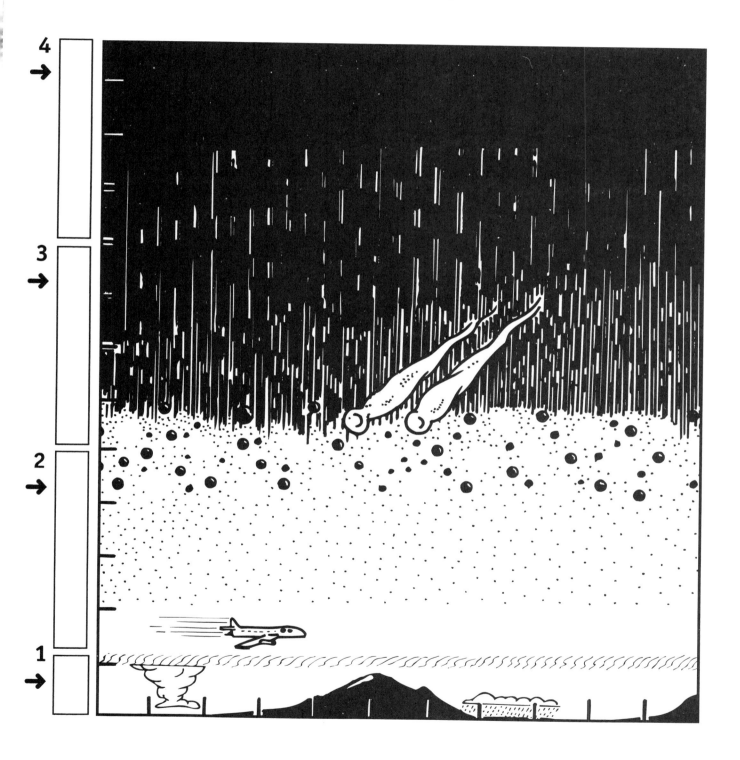

Tornado in a Bottle

Purpose:
- Observe the formation of a "tornado" due to the movement of water and air.
- Discuss why this model is representative of what occurs during a real tornado.

Materials Needed:
two 2-liter soda bottles
PVC pipe (opening fits over mouth of soda bottle)
water
rubber sealant

Procedure: See instructions on student lab sheet.

Behind the Scenes: If you live in the northern hemisphere, rotate the bottle counterclockwise to show how tornadoes spin. The rotation of the earth on its axis causes tornadoes to spin counterclockwise in that hemisphere. If you were to encounter a tornado in the southern hemisphere, it would spin clockwise.

As water from the top bottle begins to fall into the bottom bottle, it displaces the air and pushes it upward. When the bottle is shaken in a counterclockwise motion, the water molecules fall in a circular motion leaving the center column for air to quickly move into the upper bottle. Although scientists are not sure of the conditions under which a tornado occurs, it is more likely when a cold, dry air mass moves underneath a warm, moist air mass. In this case, the water represents the warm, moist air mass and the air represents the cold, dry air mass. As the lighter air mass (air in the bottle) rapidly moves up through the heavier air mass (water), a low pressure system forms in the center (column of air).

Answer Key For Questions:
1. Counterclockwise
2. Answers may vary. For example, students may answer "yes."

Literature Links:
Ganeri, A. *And Now the Weather*. Aladdin, 1992.
Gibbons, G. *Weather Forecasting*. Simon & Schuster, 1987.
Simon, S. (1987). *Storms*. Morrow, 1987.

Portals for Expansion:

Geography
- Research where "Tornado Alley" is and why this section of the United States has been given this name.

Math
- After identifying Tornado Alley, determine the average number of tornados per year. Develop a key and color code the states appropriately to show a picture graph.

Health and Safety
- Locate literature on tornado safety and discuss ways to be safe during a severe storm.

Tornado in a Bottle

Setup:

1. To make the tornado bottle, fill one of the soda bottles to the very top of the neck with water.
2. Line the inside of the PVC piping with rubber sealant and place it over the mouth of the first bottle.
3. Line the outside of the mouth of the second bottle with rubber sealant and insert the bottle mouth into the PVC piping.
4. Carefully hold the bottles upright and place in a location to dry overnight.

Preparation:

1. Holding the top bottle, begin to rotate it in a counterclockwise shaking motion. The water will begin to turn, forming a funnel-shaped column of air in the center.
2. Record your observations as to the shape of the funnel, whether or not it remains the same during the activity, and whether it stays oriented in the same direction.

Questions:

1. In which direction does the water rotate as it drains from one bottle to the other?

2. Does a "tornado" always move in the same ways from one demonstration to the next?

The Coriolis Effect

Purpose:
- Describe the rotation of the earth.
- Derive the direction of the Coriolis effect upon travel across the globe.
- Compare the Coriolis effect between the Northern and Southern Hemispheres.
- Apply the Coriolis effect to movement of air in low and high pressure areas.

Materials Needed:
markable globe
water soluble marker
ruler

Procedure:
See instructions on student lab sheet.

Answer Key For Questions:
1. Right
2. Left
3. Coriolis Effect
4. Right
5. Right
6. Counterclockwise
7. Clockwise

Literature Links:
Berger, M., & Berger, G. *How's the Weather?* Ideals Children's Books, 1993.
Ganeri, A. *And Now the Weather*. Aladdin, 1992.
Kandolan, E. *Molly's Seasons*. Cobblehill Books, 1992.

Portals for Expansion:

Language Arts
- Write to pen pals in other parts of the world to find out in what direction water drains from a full sink.

Science
- Obtain weather maps from the Internet to establish the direction of rotation of winds around low and high pressure systems.

The Coriolis Effect

Procedure: **Student Team:**

1. One student holds the globe at the poles and rotates the globe first one way and then the other.

2. Watch to see which coastline of North America becomes visible first as the globe rotates. Think about which part of your country sees the sun rise before other regions. Record your observation:
   - Circle one: East Coast or West Coast
   - The direction of rotation of the globe (earth): _____

3. One student rotates the globe in the proper direction while another holds a ruler that extends vertically toward the poles. A third student uses a water-based marker to connect the equator to the North Pole:
   - Draw in diagram "A" the marks left on the globe.
   - Place yourself at the tail of the arrow and look toward the head of the arrow and record under diagram the direction (left or right) of deflection.

4. Repeat Step 3 but draw the arrow from the equator to the South Pole:
   - Draw in the diagram "B" the marks left on the globe.
   - Place yourself at the tail of the arrow and look toward the head of the arrow and record under diagram the direction (left or right) of deflection.

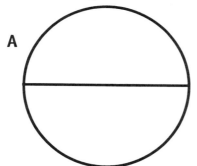

A

Northern Hemisphere:
Direction of deflection: _____

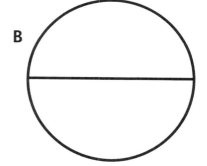

B

Southern Hemisphere:
Direction of deflection: _____

5. Repeat Step 3 but draw the arrow from the North Pole to the area near the equator. Draw and label this result in diagram "C."

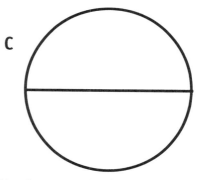

C

Northern Hemisphere:
Direction of deflection: _____

6. Repeat Step 3 but draw the arrow from the South Pole to the area near the equator. Draw and label this result in diagram "D."

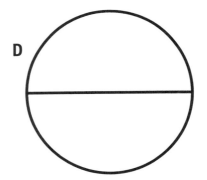

Southern Hemisphere:
Direction of deflection: _____

7. Using the deflection from the North Pole, stand at the end of each arrow below and draw the deflection that would occur as air rushes into a low pressure area. Then draw the deflection the air would experience as air rushes away from a high pressure area.

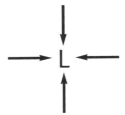 

Questions:

1. In which direction do objects appear to deflect when they move across the surface of the earth in the Northern Hemisphere?
2. In which direction do objects appear to deflect when they move across the surface of the earth in the Southern Hemisphere?
3. What is the name of this apparent deflection of the path of moving objects across the earth's surface?
4. Due to this deflection, winds in the Northern Hemisphere will tend to appear as if they are deflected to which direction?
5. As air rushes into a low pressure area, to which direction will the wind be deflected?
6. Complete the drawing of a low pressure area in Step 7 by drawing the deflection of the wind as it will occur in the Northern Hemisphere. Will the rotation of the wind around a low pressure area be clockwise or counterclockwise?
7. Complete the drawing of a high pressure area in Step 7 by drawing the deflection of the wind as it will occur in the Northern Hemisphere. Will the rotation of the wind around a high pressure area be clockwise or counterclockwise?

OCEANOGRAPHY

Fascinating Facts for Teachers

The Study of Oceanography

The ocean was, or is it the oceans were, formed as the earth cooled from its formation and water began to gather in areas of low topography over geologic time. Alternative theories do exist suggesting that the water in the ocean developed suddenly through volcanic events or a condensation of the primordial atmosphere. It is more likely, given the tremendous volume of water present in the ocean, that it accumulated there over time. How much time was required is still a mystery. Fossil evidence for an ocean exists back 2 billion years, but it is not known whether the processes of ocean formation were already taking place during the earth's formation 4.5 billion years ago. It is also clear that the composition of ocean water has remained stable for about the last 600 million years. The mysteries surrounding the origin and development of the ocean remains an important investigation for many oceanographers.

Exploration of the ocean is a young science. Pieces of the puzzle were developed throughout the centuries. Although the ancients knew their local areas fairly well for trade purposes, it was not until Ferdinand Magellan's explorations that the world was circumnavigated (1519–1522). His voyages did not reveal much about the depth of the Pacific as he used a sounding line only 200 fathoms (one fathom is 6 feet or 1.8 meters) long. Increased knowledge was represented when, in 1770, Benjamin Franklin published a map of the Gulf Stream. Great amounts of information were documented from 1831 to 1836 as the Beagle sailed and collected, among other information, oceanographic data. A young Charles Darwin formed his remarkable theories aboard that ship. Another famous expedition, the Challenger Expedition (1872–1876) gathered tremendous amounts of data about the ocean including depth, water composition, and marine life. The Meteor Expedition (1925–1927) revealed the rough terrain of the floor of the Atlantic using newly developed electronic sounding equipment. With serious uses of the ocean in both peace time and war, the total new knowledge of the ocean, its processes and characteristics, has increased dramatically.

But is there one ocean or many? Some divide the ocean into five regions: the Atlantic, Pacific, Indian, Arctic, and Antarctic Oceans. Some suggest four oceans, believing that the Antarctic Ocean is simply an extension of the Pacific, Indian, and Atlantic. Together with the Arctic, that makes four. Still others say that there are three, being the three major oceans, Atlantic, Pacific, and Indian. However, significant others, including the man whose televised explorations have made oceanography popular, Jacques-Yves Cousteau, believe that all the oceans imagined by people are false divisions. Since the waters of all comingle and affect each other, he suggests that there is only one ocean, life giving and life sustaining. This is the spirit in which this section is written. Unless otherwise specified, the ocean will refer to that single global sea that occupies nearly three-quarters of the earth's surface.

Chemical Oceanography

The main component of the ocean is water. It is a polar molecule because of its geometry. Two atoms of hydrogen are chemically bonded to an atom of oxygen, but the hydrogen atoms do not bond to sites directly opposite each other. They bond at approximately 120 degrees, not 180 degrees. Therefore, one side of the molecule tends to be dominated by the hydrogen atoms. The other side is dominated by the oxygen atom. Due to the covalent nature of the bonds between the hydrogen and the oxygen, the hydrogen side tends to carry a small positive charge, and the oxygen side a small negative charge. Because water is a polar molecule that has electrical charges not evenly distributed, it sticks well to itself (cohesion) and is seen as surface tension.

In the late seventeen hundreds, Antoine Laurent Lavoisier, famous for the discovery of oxygen, determined that water is a combination of oxygen and hydrogen. He also determined that, if the water were evaporated, ocean water left chemical material behind. He became among the first who attempted to determine what chemicals were dissolved in ocean water. The Challenger Expedition analyzed thousands of water samples. They found that dissolved oxygen decreases with depth, and that carbon dioxide increases near the surface. These facts underscore the importance of life near the surface of the ocean, although that connection was not made by the crew of the Challenger. Subsequent studies have shown that differences do occur. The average salinity of ocean water is 35 parts per thousand (grams of dissolved salt per 1000 grams of ocean water). This dissolved material makes ocean water a good conductor of electricity while pure water is not a good conductor.

See Portal for Exploration "How Much Salt Is in Ocean Water?"

See Portal for Exploration "Water on Earth"

The salinity of the ocean is affected by the hydrologic cycle. As its name implies, water is recycled and reused by the earth as water evaporates or is given off by plants and enters the atmosphere; condenses into clouds; is transported to other regions by wind; precipitates from the clouds as rain, snow, sleet or hail; and then either seeps into the ground or runs off in streams, perhaps to return again to the ocean. Ground water and stream water may contribute to the ocean in several ways. Not only do these mechanisms add water to the ocean, but they also bring dissolved materials to the ocean that adds to the chemical mix of the ocean's water. Thus, depending on the specific location of the ocean that is being discussed, the hydrologic cycle may have an impact on its chemistry. If the equatorial regions of the ocean are being discussed, then the salinity will be slightly lower as nowhere on earth is rainfall greater. This pure water acts to dilute the ocean salinity. Salinity will be lower in the vicinity of the mouth of a great river, and the salinity will be slightly higher where the rates of evaporation are very high.

Temperature also affects the density of ocean water. Where the water is warmer, the density of the ocean is less. Thus, the least dense ocean water in the

See Portal for
Exploration
"Buoyancy Activity"

world is around the equator where rain dilutes the effect of salinity and the temperature is, generally, warmest. In the polar regions, the temperatures are so very cold that even the salt water of the ocean can freeze. As it turns into "flow ice" in a process of repeated freezing and thawing, the salt crystallizes out and drops into the very cold water beneath. Thus, the water beneath the north polar ice cap is both very cold and among the most saline in the ocean. This is the most dense ocean water on earth.

The origin of the salinity of the ocean has been the subject of a great amount of investigation. It was first thought that all of the salt of the ocean was delivered to it by the rivers running across the continents. Those rivers dissolve small amounts of chemicals from the materials which they flow through and over. That dissolved material is added to the ocean along with the water in the streams. However, over geologic time, the water is evaporated to become part of the hydrologic cycle, but the dissolved materials that were carried to the ocean by those streams remain in the ocean as new dissolved material continues to be added. It now appears that volcanic activity has added significantly to the salinity of the ocean and, while the materials added to the ocean by streams remain important, volcanic activity has gained wide acceptance.

If it is true that materials are constantly being added to the ocean, a question has developed as to why salinity is not constantly increasing. An answer may have been found when large nodules containing concentrated manganese and other elements were found on the bottom of the ocean. The fact that these have formed from dissolved material in the ocean is evidence that materials will precipitate (fall out of solution) from ocean water. This process is also the origin of limestone. Dissolved chemicals brought to the ocean by streams includes calcium. The atmosphere adds carbon dioxide. Shellfish add the chemicals of their shells as the organism dies. As the concentration of these materials increases to a point that the ocean cannot hold the chemicals, they precipitate as calcium carbonate. It is believed that the limestone of the world was born through this precipitation process in the ocean. Manganese nodules are probably also a precipitate, but one where cohesive forces concentrate the chemicals involved in their formation. With all of these processes happening, the concentration of salts in the ocean remains fairly stable within a range of 33 parts per thousand to 37 parts per thousand.

Many materials are dissolved in ocean water including gasses from the atmosphere, inorganic material, organic material, and even radioactive isotopes. It is shown, and discussed above, that the ability of the ocean to use carbon dioxide in the process of creating limestone makes the ocean very important in the regulation of the global climate. Too much carbon dioxide in the atmosphere would lead to increased global warming, but the ocean is dealing with some of

106

that carbon dioxide. The concern is regarding the unknown fact of how much carbon dioxide the ocean can absorb. Additionally, there is enough gold in the ocean to fill several Fort Knox repositories. However, that material is not concentrated and recovering it is economically unrealistic. There is also enough hydrogen suitable for fusion power to power the earth and its inhabitants for, perhaps, their entire future on earth. The technology to use it lags far behind the knowledge that it exists. The promise and richness of the ocean's chemistry is great and will provide for continued development well into the future.

Physical Oceanography

The ocean is not a homogenous mixture of water. With depth, the aspects of temperature and salinity vary greatly. At the surface, the water is warm and well mixed by surface phenomenon. As depth increases, a point is reached where the temperature falls dramatically and the ocean, at great depth, becomes a very cold and inhospitable place. The water's density changes so suddenly at this point, that submarines can actually hide under this "thermocline" as sonar signals bounce off of this density change as well as off of the submarine. Salinity decreases dramatically at a "halocline" to bottom waters that remain fairly uniform in salinity. These differences, as well as differences in density described above, are among the best known dimensions of the ocean.

See Portal for Exploration "Depth and Pressure Activity"

A characteristic of water is that it is a fluid, and, as such, it exerts pressure on the surface of any object in contact with it. Water weighs 8.33 pounds per gallon (3.78 kg per 3.785 L) so that as you increase the amount of water you hold, the amount of weight increases. With surface pressure, the amount of water over you represents the amount of pressure that you would experience. Thus, the deeper you are, the more pressure you would experience. Water pressure increases one atmosphere (the weight of the atmosphere on the earth) which is 14.7 pounds (6.67 kg) on every square inch (25 mm) of every surface, for every 32.81 ft. (10 meters) in depth. Therefore after 66 ft. (20 meters) in depth, your body experiences the pressure of twice that of the atmosphere. Divers in pools know this because at deep depths, ear drums are particularly sensitive to the pressure and can hurt or even rupture. Deep diving submersibles reaching for the very deep ocean bottom can experience pressures in excess of 1000 atmospheres. Two United States submarines were lost due to the pressure of the ocean water. On April 10, 1963, the *USS Thresher* and on May 22, 1968, the *USS Scorpion* were lost off the coast of New England when pressure crushed them into oblivion.

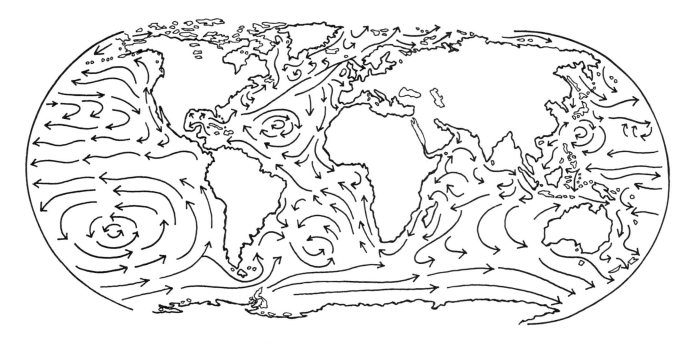

Circulation of Ocean Water

Also well known is surface ocean circulation. As wind blows across the surface of the ocean, the water "piles up" having been pushed by the pressures of the wind. The water flows in the direction of that push, but not all circulation is driven by the prevailing wind. Continents get in the way of that circulation, and a curious twist is given to moving water as it flows across the surface of the earth which is, in turn, moving itself. This effect, called the Coriolis effect, causes moving objects in the Northern Hemisphere to seem to deflect to the right of its line of movement, and in the Southern Hemisphere, the deflection is to the left. Thus, as the water moves from near the African Continent toward North America, it deflects to the right due to the combination of the obstruction of the continent and Coriolis effect. This flow is known as the Gulf Stream. Cold water flowing eastward toward Alaska deflects to the right to flow southward along the west coast of North America. Thus, the water off the Carolina Coast tends to be much warmer (coming from equatorial regions) than the waters off California (coming from subpolar regions).

See Portal for Exploration "Density Currents"

Vertical circulation in the ocean also occurs. Normal circulation of water in the Atlantic Ocean has surface water moving in the well known currents mapped by mariners, but subsurface waters also circulate. Antarctic Intermediate Water flows under the surface toward the Arctic region; it cools, falls, and may become part of the North Atlantic Deep water that flows southward underneath the Antarctic Intermediate Water. It may cool further and become part of the Antarctic Bottom Water flowing north along the very bottom of the ocean. This circulation will eventually bring even the deepest of waters back to the surface as the slow circulation of this water is completed. However, if particularly strong winds blow surface waters away, the water may be replaced by relatively cold, but nutrient rich, water from the bottom of the ocean. When this effect happens more quickly than from normal vertical circulation, it is called upwelling. Upwelling of cold water can have pronounced effects on the climate of a region, and the nutrients carried by the upwelling water can have equally pronounced effects on the marine biology of that section of the ocean.

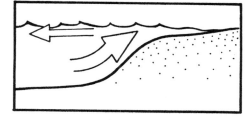

Some currents that occur on the ocean bottom may involve underwater landslides or flows of exceptionally dense water. Water with high density or water mixed with loose sediment can cause density or turbidity currents than can move downslope at high speeds creating great destruction to all ahead of them. Although no direct observations of turbidity currents have been made, indirect evidence suggests that they are another source of potential destruction that may make colonization of the ocean bottom too risky a business.

Waves are also wind generated. Although the mechanism of wave formation is not well understood, it is established that waves become larger with increased wind speed and with a larger fetch. A fetch is the area over with the wind blows. Thus, the larger an area of ocean exposed to wind, the larger the waves will become. The impetus given to water by the wind sets water into a circular motion. Important characteristics of waves include the distance from one wave crest to the next (wavelength), height of the wave, and velocity of the wave as the energy of the wave is passed through water. It is important to remember that waves do not move water in the ocean. Ocean circulation does. Waves do not really move water until the wave enters a shallow region where the circulation pattern being transmitted by the wave is interrupted by the bottom, and the wave form gains height, pitches forward and breaks. As any surfer knows, a breaking wave does throw water upon the beach.

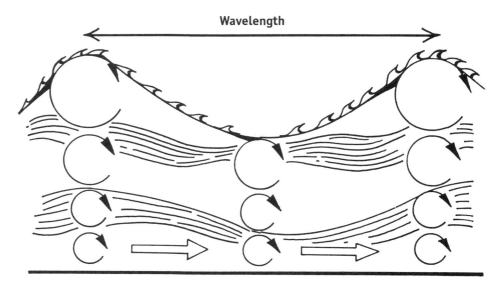

How Ocean Water Moves

See Portal for Exploration "Wave Action"   The water thrown onto a beach must return to the line of breakers. The mechanism that does this is called an undercurrent or undertow. The water thrown onto the beach flows across the bottom under any new breaking waves, allowing no accumulation of water on the beach. The motion of this water can be felt as sand is drawn from under the foot of anyone standing in the water where breakers are creating surf. Once beyond the line of breakers, this effect is not felt. Being caught in a normal undertow or normal wave action is not as dangerous as we might believe. Another effect is much greater. If onshore winds and wave action are acting to pile ocean water against a beach area, that water must return to the ocean. The mechanism that causes this to happen is called a rip current or rip tide. The rip current flowing at several miles (or kilometers) per hour can move a great deal of water into the ocean several miles (or kilometers) from the beach. This is faster than a swimmer can swim, and can represent a challenging distance for most swimmers. Rip currents are narrow, and rather than trying to swim against the current, swimmers should move parallel to the beach until the beach is no longer retreating. Once the swimmer is out of the rip current, swimming toward the beach can be successful.

Some waves are capable of high amounts of destruction. The very high wind and related push of water supplied by large storms can create a storm surge. These are responsible for much of the damage due to flooding and high water related to hurricanes and other large storms. In 1900, 6000 people drowned in Galveston due to just such an effect. Especially in earthquake prone areas, large masses of rock can suddenly enter the sea. These landslide surges are particularly dangerous in restricted bodies of water. In 1958 a strong earthquake caused a landslide, and a resulting landslide surge in Lituya Bay, Alaska. The landslide surge grew to 500 meters as it washed up the opposite side of the bay destroying all in its wake.

The greatest of the destructive waves is the tsunami, named for the Japanese word for seismic sea wave. A tsunami is caused when undersea earthquakes displace the sea bottom and cause the cyclic motion seen at the surface as a wave. As a tsunami moves across the open ocean, most of the wave travels under the surface and may be undetectable to a ship steaming over it. As the wave moves into a shallow area, it slows trading its kinetic energy of motion for potential energy as its height grows. Tsunamis can travel across the ocean at speeds in excess of 300 miles (482.7 km) per hour and may, as observed during a Hawaiian event, wash inland to 65.6 ft. (20 meters) above sea level. Systems of seismic observatories are now in place and will issue tsunami warnings if such an event appears likely.

One wave, not often thought of as a wave, is the twice daily rise and fall of the ocean called the tide. Tidal effects are caused primarily by the gravitational effects of the moon. As the gravity of the moon pulls on the earth, it is thought that the water is more easily pulled from the near side than the solid rock of the earth. On the side of the earth opposite the moon, the gravity of the moon has acted on the entire mass of the earth pulling the rock toward the moon more than the water at this increased distance. Thus, at any time, there are two areas with deeper water, by several feet, than at other points. In addition, the extra water must come from someplace, which is the areas between the high tides. Thus, as the earth rotates, the ocean will pass through two areas of high tide, and two areas of low tide.

See Portal for Exploration "Tides and Tidal Bores"

Approximately twice each lunar month, the gravity of the moon and the sun are lined up (the new and full moon phases). On these days, the high tides are particularly high and are called the spring tide. If the high tides are exceptionally high, this must be a time when the low tides are exceptionally low, with much of the water going to the ocean to build the high tides. Also twice a month, the gravity of the moon and sun act on the earth at a right angle. The sun tries to build a tide where the moon is borrowing water for its high tide. During this period (the first and last quarter phases of the moon), the high tides are at their lowest point, and the low tides are the highest. Sometimes, the increased amount of water is funneled by a bay or estuary, and the increase in water depth can be seen as an actual wave form advancing up the estuary. These tidal bores can be nearly 10 feet (3 m) high and move at 15 miles (24 km) per hour.

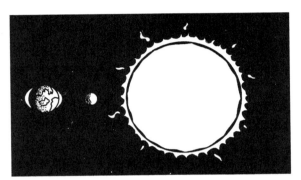

Sun, Earth, Moon Positions During Tides

Geological Oceanograhy

Even the definition of an ocean is tied to the science of geology. An ocean is a body of salt water, partially surrounded by continents, and underlain by SIMA. SIMA is a term that needs explanation. When the world was first forming, a layer of material, high in silicon and magnesium (SIMA) formed a skin, called the crust, around the cooling earth. Less dense pockets of still molten SIAL material (silicon and aluminum) later came together, cooled, and formed the topographic high areas we now know as continents. While the SIMA can be found underneath the SIAL pockets that became the continents, the crust of the earth underneath the ocean is also SIMA material. More dense and basaltic than the lighter granite-like material of the continents, SIMA is the true ocean bottom. If one examines a globe of the earth, it can easily be seen that every major ocean division (Atlantic, Pacific, and Indian, is surrounded, in part, by the continental masses of SIAL that hardened on top of the SIMA crust. Thus, the true ocean bottom is significantly different from the continents.

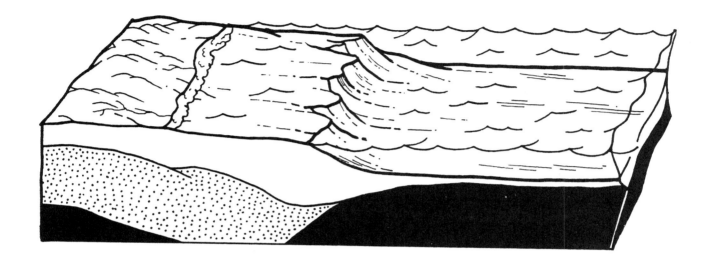

During World War II, the use of sound to test the depth of the ocean was developed. Originally a defensive device to locate submarines, sonar was used to "sound" the depth of the ocean for exploration rather than using a weighted line. The electronic sounding of the ocean provided some startling and unexpected surprises. The topography of the ocean bottom is much greater than the topography of terrestrial systems exposed to the wearing away forces of weathering and erosion. Very high mountains and very deep valleys occur in seemingly random patterns. Until advances were made in understanding how the crust of the earth is made and destroyed, the random locations of deep ocean phenomenon were seen as just that—phenomenon. In terms of plate tectonics, the topography becomes a little more understandable.

The zones where tectonic plates are spreading apart are, very often, found under the sea. These submarine spreading zones cause a line of volcanic mountains 25,000 miles long. This chain of volcanic mountains called the mid-ocean ridge, has a very long rift running down the central, and highest, section of the mountain. This fissure, volcanically active, represents the site where tectonic plates pull apart, leaving a gap filled with material erupting from beneath the surface. This is the birthplace of new crustal material and is basaltic in nature, or made of SIMA material. The spreading has continued over time, and if a physiographic globe is consulted, one can easily imagine how the midocean ridge has pushed the Americas and Africa apart as they ride as SIAL passengers on the SIMA tectonic plates.

See Portal for Exploration "Mapping the Ocean Floor"

As the plates are pushed apart, they must encounter each other at some other point. Where they do, the plates may collide and buckle upward into huge mountain chains. This is the manner in which the Himalayas were built. At other locations, one plate may override the other forcing the later to dive to destruction in the mantle, perhaps to be recycled at some other time as new crustal material. But as the plate dives into the mantle, it drags neighboring material down with it, thus creating long, very thin, deep gashes in the ocean bottom. These gashes are called trenches, and are the locations of the deepest spots of all. In the Mariana Trench, a spot known as the Challenger Deep is over 7 miles (11.26 km) deep. This is a greater vertical distance in depth from sea level than the distance represented by the earth's highest mountain peaks from sea level.

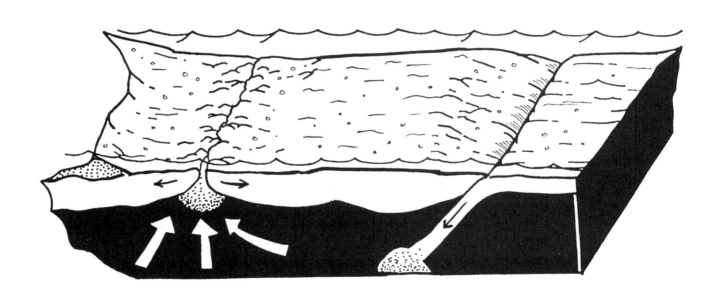

Other phenomenon include island arcs. As a tectonic plate moves over a hot spot in the mantle, a chain of volcanoes can punch through the thin SIMA ocean bottom to create a chain of islands. The chain will be stretched out becoming a tell-tale for the direction of the movement of the crust as the plate carries the islands with it. One of the most famous of these arcs is the Hawaiian Islands that continues to grow both in size from active volcanism and in number as new islands continue to be born in underwater birthplaces.

It is also true that the level of the ocean varies over time by both the lifting and falling of the land, and by great ice ages tying up water that may have otherwise been part of the ocean. Volcanoes that grow from the ocean bottom are often ringed by coral reefs. As the volcano is worn away, or as it falls away by a rising sea level or a receding ocean bottom, the coral may hold its level in the warm shallows. Many such structures are seen in the South Pacific, and are called atolls. One of the most famous of these is the Bikini Atoll, location of the first hydrogen bomb explosion, and home to a society that inspired a fashionable type of bathing suit.

  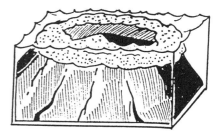

The fact that the sea levels have changed is also visible in the variety of types of coastlines. The smooth beaches of the mid-Atlantic coast and related barrier islands would indicate that the bottom of the ocean, and its related sand structures, have emerged to create, at least temporarily, terrestrial features. Beaches and barrier islands from New Jersey to Florida are features of emergent shorelines. However, the steep-sided valleys leading to narrow beaches of Maine are evidence that mountain valleys can fall away under the weight of glaciers to become flooded. The rough terrain of Maine, and the lines of islands that protrude from irregular coastlines are features of submergent shorelines. Nothing, however, remains the same, and with the melting of the great glaciers, it may be that the state of Maine will slowly rise and the flooded valleys may drain, while the New Jersey area may drop in a balancing event, to once again become part of the ocean bottom.

Portals for Learning: Literature

Armentrout, P. *Ocean Currents*. Rourke Press, 1996.
Traces background information on ocean currents. The book also discusses how ocean currents were mapped, the reason they continue moving, and their affect on weather. A glossary is provided.

Armentrout, P. *Waves and Tides*. Rourke Press, 1996.
This book provides the reader with information on waves and tides. It explains how waves are caused and what happens when earthquakes and volcanoes occur causing larger destructive waves.

Bannan, J. G. *Sand Dunes*. Carolrhoda Books, 1989.
Although not totally related to the ocean, this book explains how sand dunes are formed and the forces that act upon them. The book provides line diagrams along with photographs of different types of sand dunes. A glossary and index are provided.

Blassingame, W. *The First Book of the Seashore*. Franklin Watts, 1964.
This older book provides a vast amount of information relating to the ocean and seashore. It discusses topics such as the origin of the oceans, life found in and around the ocean, and the coastline and shores.

Bramwell, M. *The Oceans*. Franklin Watts, 1987.
An encyclopedia-type book, this is an excellent reference for reading about the ocean. It covers a vast amount of material from the ocean currents to tides to exploring the deep. Each topic is given a two-page explanation that uses both diagrams and realistic pictures to explain the points.

Carter, K. J. *Oceans*. Children's Press, 1982.
Written for younger students, this book provides information on the world's oceans. It provides real photos and excellent diagrams that help explain its information. The ocean floor, surface, shore, tides, and currents are all covered in this book.

Conley, A. *Window on the Deep: The Adventures of Underwater Explorer Sylvia Earle*. Franklin Watts, 1991.
Traces the explorations of Sylvia Earle. The book provides real-life photographs of deep sea submersibles, exploration equipment, and procedures for exploring the mysterious ocean floor. The book also gives a brief history of diving.

Doubilet, A. *Under the Sea from A to Z*. Crown, 1991.
This book takes each letter of the alphabet and provides a wonderful colored picture of a form of sea life that begins with that letter. Although related to life science, this book gives excellent pictures of surrounding features in the ocean.

Fernandes, E. *The Little Boy Who Cried Himself to Sea*. Kids Can Press, 1982.
As a little child cries himself to sleep, he finds that he is carried to the ocean and begins to drift. Ocean creatures keep careful watch until his mother tows him back to the shore.

Henry, B. *Water*. Roy Publications, 1968.

Although dated, the book provides black and white photographs that explain uses of water throughout the world. This book would serve as a good reference for older students who are researching about water.

Holsaert, E., & Holseart, F. *Ocean Wonders*. Holt Rinehart and Winston, 1965.

This book highlights general information about the ocean. It begins by discussing how the ocean is explored using deep sea explorers, and continues by looking at resources found in the ocean.

Kinney, J., & Kinney, C. *What Does the Tide Do?* Young Scott Books, 1966.

A story of a little boy named Damon who sits and watches as the tide comes in at the Massachusetts shore. During his adventure, he catches a fish with the help of an old fisherman who explains why the sea is rising, and that it will eventually recede. There is an explanation at the end of the book that explains why the tide rises and falls.

Mariner, T. *Oceans*. Marshall Cavendish, 1990.

This book explores the physical characteristics of the oceans along with their interaction and relationship to each other. Gives excellent diagrams and drawings that aid the reader in understanding the information provided.

Sandak, C. R. *The World's Oceans*. Franklin Watts, 1987.

Written for older students, this book highlights the history of early oceanography through today's means of exploring the ocean. It also includes information on deep sea submersibles and future exploration of the world's oceans. A dateline is provided.

Smith, B. E. *The Seashore Book*. Houghton Mifflin, 1985.

Two children discover how the seashore industry works as they spend a summer vacation with a captain on the coast. Would serve as a good reference for discussing trade on the ocean.

Stone, A. H., & Ingmanson, D. *Crystals from the Sea: A Look at Salt*. Prentice-Hall, 1969.

This book looks at the many uses of salt and also discusses physical characteristics such as density, solubility, and conductivity. The book could be useful when discussing saltwater.

Taylor, B. (1993). *Rivers and Oceans*. Kingfisher Books, 1993.

This factual book discusses the ways water is found within our world and the water cycle. It is useful for oceanography, highlighting and presenting information on ocean currents, waves, and tides.

Water on Earth

Teacher Demonstration

Purpose: • Describe where water is found on the earth, its states of matter, and its distribution.

Materials Needed:
globe or large map of the earth   calculator
37.9 L (10 gallon) aquarium   measuring containers
19.95 L (5 gallons) water

Introduction: The water we have on the earth is the same water we had when the earth formed. It continues through a cycle where it is heated causing evaporation, cooled resulting in condensation, and then falls back to earth as precipitation, running off into a river, stream, or lake. Although 70% of the earth's surface is covered by water, a very small percentage of that water is consumable or usable for humans. The saltwater found in the world's oceans comprises 97% of the water on the earth.

Procedure:
1. Discuss the earth's water resources. Show a map or globe of the earth to aid the discussion.
2. Have the students estimate how much of the earth's surface is covered by water and more specifically the earth's oceans.
3. Discuss possible uses for ocean water, arriving at a conclusion regarding its consumability for humans.
4. Place the aquarium with water in front of the students and explain that this represents all of the water on the earth.
5. Take out the water that represents the ocean water. This can be done by taking out the relative percentage of water: 97.2% of the water is 18.4 L (622.08 fl oz).
6. Involve the students in a discussion regarding the water found in the ocean and the amount of life it supports. Have the students draw a bar graph or chart to show where water is found on the earth and the representative amounts.

Behind the Scenes: The total amount of water found on the earth is divided among different locations such as the oceans, lakes, rivers, streams, icebergs, etc. The following percentages represent how much is located in each place: oceans–97.2%, icecaps and glaciers–2.0%, groundwater 0.62%, freshwater lakes–0.009%, inland seas/salt lakes–0.008%, atmosphere–0.001%, all rivers–0.0001%.

Literature Links:
Bramwell, M. *The Oceans.* Franklin Watts, 1987.
Carter, K. J. *Oceans.* Children's Press, 1982.
Henry, B. *Water.* Roy Publications, 1968.
Mariner, T. *Oceans.* Marshall Cavendish, 1990.
Taylor, B. *Rivers and Oceans.* Kingfisher Books, 1993.

Portals for Expansion:
Mathematics
• Repeat the demonstration. Give the students the percentages and have them determine how much water should be taken out for each location/type of water found on the earth.
• Using ratios, estimate how much of the water on earth is freshwater, saltwater, glaciers, and held by the atmosphere as humidity.
Social Studies
• Using an atlas and large wall map determine which inland bodies of water are freshwater and which are saltwater. Place identifying flags or pushpins on each water body.
• Discuss options for obtaining freshwater for those places where it is in short supply.

Buoyancy

Purpose:
- Define buoyancy in terms of floating and sinking by explaining the activity.
- Apply knowledge of bouyancy to salinity in the ocean by answering questions posed as part of the activity.

Materials Needed:
plastic glass (large enough to hold an egg)   salt
hard-boiled egg   spoon
water

Procedure: See instructions on student lab sheet.

Answer Key For Questions:
1. Answers will vary. For example, salt was added to the water.
2. The egg sinks. The water is less dense.
3. The water sinks. The egg is less dense.
4. No
5. Saltwater
6. Answers will vary. For example, The water with a high salt content will tend to sink in a deep ocean system.
7. Answers will vary. For example, the submarine will sink to a lower depth.

Literature Links:
Bramwell, M. *The Oceans*. Franklin Watts, 1987.
Carter, K. J. *Oceans*. Children's Press, 1982.
Conley, A. *Window on the Deep: The Adventures of Underwater Explorer Sylvia Earle*. Franklin Watts, 1991.
Fernandes, E. *The Little Boy Who Cried Himself to Sea*. Kids Can Press, 1982.
Holsaert, E., & Holseart, F. *Ocean Wonders*. Holt, Rinehart and Winston, 1965.
Mariner, T. *Oceans*. Marshall Cavendish, 1990.
Sandak, C. R. *The World's Oceans*. Franklin Watts, 1987.
Stone, A. H., & Ingmanson, D. *Crystals from the Sea: A Look at Salt*. Prentice-Hall, 1969.

Portals for Expansion:

Social Studies
- Write a report that describes what icebergs are, why they float, and how they were involved in the sinking of the Titanic.
- Have students sort plastic items from waste and identify which items may be mistaken for floating jellyfish by ocean creatures who feed on them.

Science
- Do an experiment that tests what materials sink or float in freshwater, and whether or not they sink or float in saltwater.

Language Arts
- Have students write stories about things discarded by others that they might find floating in the ocean.

Art
- Draw a picture or produce a work of art representing an object that is floating in, or that has sunk to the depths of the ocean.

Bouyancy

Procedure: **Trial 1**

1. Fill the plastic glass about two-thirds with water.
2. Place the hard-boiled egg into the glass.
3. Write/draw your observations of what happens to the egg in this water.
4. Take out the hard-boiled egg.

Trial 2

5. Add several spoonfuls of salt to the water and stir to dissolve the salt.
6. Again place the egg in the saltwater.
7. Write/draw your observations of what happens to the egg in this water.
8. Take out the hard-boiled egg.

Trial 1: Draw what the egg, glass, and water look like. Explain your drawing.	Trial 2: Draw what the egg, glass, and saltwater look like. Explain your drawing.

Questions: *Answer the questions on the back of the paper.*

1. What changes did you make that may have caused the different results in the trials?
2. In Trial 1, what is more dense and sinks? What is less dense and floats?
3. In Trial 2, what is more dense and sinks? What is less dense and floats?
4. Did you change the egg in any way that would make it more or less dense?
5. What is more dense, freshwater or saltwater?
6. What kind of water would tend to sink in a deep ocean system, water with a lot of salt content or water with low salt content?
7. As a submarine passes from very salty water to water that has less salt, will the submarine tend more to sink or float?

How Much Salt Is in Ocean Water?

Purpose:
- Determine the salt content of ocean water using evaporation as a mechanism in the activity.
- Properly use lab equipment, including a triple beam balance and a beaker.

Materials Needed:
400 mL beaker
250 mL graduated cylinder
triple beam balance
ocean water (simulated)
dropper

Preparation:
Make simulated ocean water by dissolving 35 grams of table salt in 965 grams (965 mL) of water. The salinity of ocean water varies between 33 to 37 parts per thousand. This recipe represents the average of those extremes.

Special Instructions:
If needed, see page 34 for instructions in using the triple beam balance for measuring the mass of the empty beaker and the mass of the beaker with salt residue. When filling the cylinder with 250 mL of water, use a dropper to add or subtract water until an exact amount is obtained. *Remember:* Read the volume of the water in the graduated cylinder by looking at the side and reading the number at the bottom of the meniscus. The meniscus is the top surface of the water in the graduated cylinder. The bottom of the meniscus should be even with the 250 mL reading.

Procedure:
See instructions on student lab sheet.

Answer Key For Questions:
1. Answers will vary. For example, salt was left behind in the container.
2. Answers will vary. For example, the additional mass is the salt that was added.
3. Answers will vary but expectations can be on the order of 37 parts salt per thousand.

Literature Links:
Blassingame, W. *The First Book of the Seashore.* Franklin Watts, 1964.
Bramwell, M. *The Oceans.* Franklin Watts, 1987.
Carter, K. J. *Oceans.* Children's Press, 1982.
Fernandes, E. *The Little Boy Who Cried Himself to Sea.* Kids Can Press, 1982.
Mariner, T. *Oceans.* Marshall Cavendish, 1990.
Stone, A. H., & Ingmanson, D. *Crystals from the Sea: A Look at Salt.* Prentice-Hall, 1969.

Portals for Expansion:

Social Studies
- Using a map, and information received from salt companies, locate large salt deposits to find out where great oceans once stood.
- Do research to find what people still obtain their salt by evaporating ocean water.

Language Arts
- Write to Morton Salt Company to find out where and how ionized salt is processed.
- Write to Akzo Salt Company to find out where and how they get their salt used to melt ice on roads.

How Much Salt Is in Ocean Water?

Procedure:
1. Determine the mass of the beaker at the start of the activity. Record it below.
2. Measure out 250 mL of simulated ocean water using a graduated cylinder.
3. Pour the contents of the graduated cylinder into the beaker.
4. Place the beaker in a spot where the water will evaporate, such as near a heater or on a sunny windowsill. All of the water should evaporate in one or two days.
5. During each day, make observations and record them in the space below. Describe or draw pictures.
6. Determine the mass of the beaker with the residue when the water has evaporated.
7. Calculate the mass of the salt in the ocean water by subtracting the mass of the beaker from the mass of the beaker and residue.
8. Multiple the mass of the salt in your sample by four to find out the average salinity found in 1000 grams of ocean water.

What is the mass of the beaker and residue? _____ grams

What is the mass of the beaker at the start? — _____ grams

Amount of salt _____ grams

What is the amount of salt in your sample? _____ grams

Multiply by four to find average salinity. X   4

Average salinity of the ocean per 1000 grams _____ grams

Observations:

Questions: *Answer the questions on the back of the paper.*
1. Why did the beaker have more mass after the water evaporated?
2. Where did this additional mass come from?
3. Based on your calculations, describe what your answer means in terms of the average salinity of ocean water.

Depth and Pressure

Purpose:
- Describe the relationship between depth and pressure by drawing results of the activity.
- Speculate on how the activity relates to increasing depths in the ocean environment.

Materials Needed:
plastic 2-liter bottle
water
cap or stopper for the bottle
tub or large sink full of water
incense

Preparation:
1. Take all labeling off a 2-liter bottle. If the bottle has a separate base, that, also, can be removed by pulling it off the bottle.
2. Put three marks on the bottle so that it is separated into four sections.
3. Create three holes in the bottle, nearly, but not exactly, one above the other.

Procedure:
See instructions on student lab sheet.

Behind the Scenes:
For this activity, it is suggested that a lit stick of incense be used to create very small, but perfectly round, smooth holes in the plastic of the bottle. Be sure to have an adult retain control of the hot object so that no lit ends fall off to create a risk of fire or be mishandled increasing the risk of burn injury.

Answer Key For Questions:
1. Lowest
2. Pressure increases with depth
3. Bottom

Literature Links:
Armentrout, P. *Ocean Currents*. Rourke Press, 1996.
Bramwell, M. *The Oceans*. Franklin Watts, 1987.
Carter, K. J. *Oceans*. Children's Press, 1982.
Conley, A. *Window on the Deep: The Adventures of Underwater Explorer Sylvia Earle*. Franklin Watts, 1991.
Holsaert, E., & Holseart, F. *Ocean Wonders*. Holt, Rinehart and Winston, 1965.
Mariner, T. *Oceans*. Marshall Cavendish, 1990.

Portals for Expansion:

Social Studies
- Compose a news story that covers the loss of the *USS Thresher* or *Scorpion*. Students may be interested in researching how other ships have been lost at sea or in the Great Lakes area.

Science
- Investigate the shape of deep sea submersibles to find what shape is best to withstand the pressure of the ocean.
- Create a time line of ocean exploration using deep sea submersibles.

Language Arts
- Write a report on the dangers presented to divers who harvest sponges or oysters from the ocean bottom.

Depth and Pressure

Procedure:

1. Put the bottle into the tub or sink so that water completely fills the bottle.
2. While holding the bottle under water, put the cap tightly on the bottle.
3. Cover the top two holes with your fingers.
4. Bring the bottle out of the water, holding the bottle so that when the holes are uncovered, the water will leak into the tub or sink.
5. Uncover the holes, and observe what happens.
6. Draw what happens when the water is allowed to flow from the bottle:

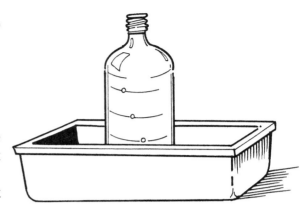

Explain your drawing:

Questions:

1. From which hole does water squirt the farthest?

2. What does that tell you about the relationship of depth to pressure?

3. Is pressure greatest at the ocean's surface or at the ocean's bottom?

Density Currents

Purpose: • Observe how a density current moves.

Materials Needed: cooler
ice

Each group:

plastic shoe box	water
baby food jar	salt
food coloring	wood block

Introduction: Saltwater is more dense than freshwater since there is more matter packed into the same amount of space. Additionally, cold water is more dense than warmer water. Density currents exist because as water cools it sinks towards the bottom of the ocean floor similar to the way clouds form. Cold water sinks and pushes warmer water towards the surface as it replaces the warmer water. Patterns of currents develop that run from the poles towards the equator.

Preparation: Several hours prior to the lab, dissolve the salt into a large container of water. After the salt has been dissolved, color the water with the food coloring. Fill baby food jars with the saltwater, then seal the jars before placing them into a cooler of ice.

Procedure: Begin a discussion by asking the students if they ever sit on the floor in their living room. Ask them what happens in the winter when someone opens the door. Where do they feel the cold air first? Explain that since cold air is more dense than warm air, cold air sinks and replaces the warmer air, pushing it upwards. The same thing happens with water.

See instructions on student lab sheet for further explanation.

Behind the Scenes: Ocean water on the average has 35 parts of dissolved salt per 1000 parts of water. However it varies in different places. One of these places is near the poles. When ocean water freezes, only freshwater ice forms, thus causing the salt to be left and increasing the salinity of the water. This is one reason why density currents originate in polar regions and flow towards the equator.

Answer Key For Questions:
1. Answers will vary. For example, the cold water ran across the bottom of the box.
2. Answers will vary. For example, cold water is more dense.
3. Answers will vary. For example: Near the equator the salt content is higher due to evaporation. This increases the salinity causing the surface water to sink. Near the polar regions the surface water sinks.
4. Answers will vary. For example, the warm water is forced up and a convection current could be formed.

Literature Links: Armentrout, P. *Ocean Currents*. Rourke Press, 1996.
Armentrout, P. *Waves and Tides*. Rourke Press, 1996.
Sandak, C. R. *The World's Oceans*. Franklin Watts, 1987.

Portals for Expansion: **Social Studies**
• Obtain a ocean chart that illustrates the density of cold water currents and compare those to trade currents used by explorers.

Density Currents

Procedure: 1. Fill the plastic shoe box approximately one-quarter full with room temperature water. Prop the box under one end with a wood block. The entire bottom of the container should be covered with at least 2 cm of water at the shallow end.
2. Obtain a baby food jar from your teacher.
3. Carefully and slowly pour the cold salt water from the baby food jar into the shoe box along one end and observe the movement of the cold water as it flows into the water.
4. Describe how the cold water moves in the diagram provided.

Be sure to label the direction the water moved.

Questions: 1. What happened to the cold water when you poured it into the shoe box?

2. Why do you think this happened?

3. The colored water also contained dissolved salt which made it denser than the water in the shoe box. Describe where on the earth the ocean water has more salt and what should happen at these points.

4. As the cold water entered the container, what did it do to the warm water? Describe how a cycle will occur after time.

Wave Action

Purpose:
- Identify characteristics and terms relating to ocean waves including wavelength, period, height, velocity, and fetch.
- Establish relationships between wind speed and fetch and the general characteristics of waves.
- Observe and identify the conditions that must be present for longshore currents.

Materials Needed:
multi-speed desk fan
oblong pan
water
ruler
small Styrofoam "peanuts"
small wood block
watch with second hand or stopwatch

Procedure:
See instructions on student lab sheet.

This activity can easily be repeated by varying the conditions, such as changing the depth of the water or the speed of the fan.

Answer Key For Questions:
1. Answers will vary. For example: Yes. Shallow water has higher waves.
2. Answers will vary greatly.
3. Answers will vary. For example, sand is moved along the beach.

Literature Links:
Armentrout, P. *Ocean Currents*. Rourke Press, 1996.
Armentrout, P. *Waves and Tides*. Rourke Press, 1996.
Bramwell, M. *The Oceans*. Franklin Watts, 1987.
Carter, K. J. *Oceans*. Children's Press, 1982.
Conley, A. *Window on the Deep: The Adventures of Underwater Explorer Sylvia Earle*. Franklin Watts, 1991.
Kinney, J., & Kinney, C. *What Does the Tide Do?* Young Scott Books, 1966.

Portals for Expansion:

Language Arts
- Write a story about being at the beach and watching or listening to the waves as they break on the beach.

Music
- Listen to a "nature recording" of waves crashing on the beach, and discuss the feelings and emotions the recording evokes.

Wave Action

Procedure: 1. Set up the equipment as shown in the diagram.

2. Put water into the pan so that nearly the entire bottom is covered. Some of the shallow end should not be covered by water.
3. Clean up any spills.
4. Turn on the fan at its lowest speed.
5. Put the ruler into the deep end of the water to measure the difference in the depth of the water as a wave passes by the ruler. Record this in the chart below.
6. Put the ruler at the shallow end where the waves "break" on the bottom of the pan. Measure the difference in the wave height at this point. Record in the chart on the next page.
7. Hold the ruler parallel to and over the water surface, then measure the difference between high points in the waves, or crests.
8. Record the distance between two wave crests as the wavelength.
9. Time the travel of a wave over 20 cm.
10. Turn off the fan.
11. Using the example below, calculate how far the wave would travel in one second.

$$\frac{20 \text{ cm}}{\text{time measurement}} \; = \; \underline{\hspace{2cm}} \text{ per second}$$

12. Multiply 20 cm by 1 second. Divide by your time measurement. Record this distance as the wave velocity per second.
13. Place the fan so that the air strikes the pan at an angle.

Name

14. Place several Styrofoam "peanuts" along the water's edge.
15. Turn on the fan.
16. Record your observations as to what happens to the "peanuts."
17. Try to take the measurements of wave height, wavelength, and velocity at another speed of the fan. Record the information in the chart below.
18. Try to take the measurements of wave height, wavelength, and velocity at another depth of water. Record the information in the chart below.

	Initial Set-up	Higher Fan Speed	Deeper Water
Wave height in deep water			
Wave height at the shallow end			
Wave length of the waves			
Wave velocity			

Observations: What happens to the peanuts if the waves break on shore at an angle?

Questions: *Answers the questions on the back of the paper.*
1. Is there a difference between wave height where the water is deep and where the water is shallow?
2. Is there a difference in wavelength between conditions on low wind speed and high wind speed?
3. When waves approach a shoreline at an angle, it causes a "longshore current." Just like your "peanuts," what do you think is the effect of a longshore current on the sand of the beach?

Tides and Tidal Bores

Purpose:
- Explain how a tide acts as a wave and grows as it nears the shoreline.
- Apply the principle of focusing a wave's energy by creating a model of a tidal bore.

Materials Needed:
clear plastic pan or plastic shoe box
ruler
water
protractor

Introduction: In the deep mid-ocean, the tide will change sea level only very slightly. It is not until the tide "wave" nears the shoreline that the height of the wave increases to the familiar and rhythmic change we see at the beach or in rivers and bays affected by the tide. The tide sloshes on the shore much as the water sloshes against the side of the container. A tide "wave" may act differently if it enters a closed bay that narrows as it moves away from the ocean. The water enters a wide mouth and, as it proceeds up the bay, is forced into a smaller area as the bay narrows. This is capable of causing a relatively high tide "wave" that can wash up the bay in a visible wave front. These "tidal bores" are modeled by the effect as the water in the container sloshes into a corner of the container.

Procedure: See instructions on student lab sheet.

Answer Key For Questions:
1. Answers will vary. For example, the tide changes the most in a corner where the available space narrows.
2. Answers will vary. For example, the tide grows the highest along the edges of the pan.
3. Answers will vary. For example, the tide grows the least in the middle of the pan.

Literature Links:
Armentrout, P. *Ocean Currents*. Rourke Press, 1996.
Armentrout, P. *Waves and Tides*. Rourke Press, 1996.
Bramwell, M. *The Oceans*. Franklin Watts, 1987.
Kinney, J., & Kinney, C. *What Does the Tide Do?* Young Scott Books, 1966.
Sandak, C. R. *The World's Oceans*. Franklin Watts, 1987.

Portals for Expansion:

Mathematics
- Calculate the ratio between the high and shallow depths as observed in the container in the middle, on the side, and in the corner.

Language Arts
- Write a story about the kinds of ships that use tides to enter and leave a bay or harbor in your region. Include details about the cargo being delivered or ready for transport.

Name

Tides and Tidal Bores

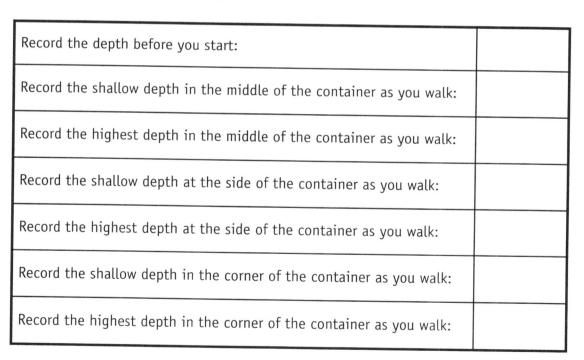

Procedure:

1. Put about 25 mm of water in the clear plastic container.
2. Measure the water's depth by vertically placing a ruler in the middle of the pan. Record the depth.
3. Walk across the room holding the container. Have your partner observe how the water moves.
4. Record how the depth changes in terms of the lowest and highest measurements.
5. Next, walk across the room while your partner measures the change in depth at the side of the container.
6. Next, hold the container turned at a 45° angle so that a corner is near your body and a corner points in the direction of movement.
7. Carry the container across the room while your partner measures the change in depth in the corner of the container.

Record the depth before you start:	
Record the shallow depth in the middle of the container as you walk:	
Record the highest depth in the middle of the container as you walk:	
Record the shallow depth at the side of the container as you walk:	
Record the highest depth at the side of the container as you walk:	
Record the shallow depth in the corner of the container as you walk:	
Record the highest depth in the corner of the container as you walk:	

Questions: *Answer the questions on the back of the paper.*

1. Where does the "tide" change the most?
2. Where does the "tide" grow the highest?
3. Where does the "tide" change the least?

Mapping the Ocean Floor

Purpose:
- Construct a grid that represents what the bottom of your ocean floor model looks like by obtaining depth measurements and plotting them.
- Interpret the grid when constructed and identify features found on the ocean floor.

Materials Needed:

| plastic shoe box for each ocean floor | Exacto knife | graph paper |
| modeling clay | ruler | |

Introduction: Older maps of the ocean floor were made by dropping a lead weight on a string into the water and measuring the depth when it came to the bottom. This method was done over and over again until a map of the ocean floor originated. Current scientists map the ocean floor by using echo sounding which bounces a sound off of the ocean floor and constructs a map based on the time it takes to get the echo. Students in this activity will map the ocean floor using the old method and construct a grid that depicts what the ocean floor will look like.

Procedure:
1. Have each group of students construct an ocean floor by forming modeling clay in the bottom of a plastic shoe box. Paint the outside of the box to prevent others from viewing the terrain.
2. Prepare the box lid or piece of cardboard by cutting slits into it. Be sure the slits are large enough for a ruler to slip through them.
3. See student lab sheet for further instructions.

Answer Key For Questions:
1. Answers will vary. For example, parts of the ocean floor include the continental shelf, continental slope, trenches, seamounts, flat-topped hills, and ocean basin.
2. Answers will vary.
3. Answers will vary. For example: No. It slopes downward in all directions.

Behind the Scenes: This activity will only give you one reading for each point whereas when the ocean floor is mapped, hundreds of readings around a point are taken in order to get a true depiction of the topographical features. You can extend this activity for older students by making two or three cuts for each point and have them determine the ocean floor in more detail.

Literature Links: Blassingame, W. *The First Book of the Seashore*. Franklin Watts, 1964.
Bramwell, M. *The Oceans*. Franklin Watts, 1987.
Carter, K. J. *Oceans*. Children's Press, 1982.
Mariner, T. *Oceans*. Marshall Cavendish, 1990.

Portals for Expansion:

Math
- Take more readings and graph them on the chart. Determine a mean reading for the profile.
- Construct models of the ocean floor that could be connected. After each group maps their ocean, connect the maps to obtain a longer ocean floor depiction.

Language Arts
- Pretend that students are ancient explorers who are on an assignment to map the ocean floor. Have them send letters home on parchment type paper describing their adventures.

LAB
Oceanography

Mapping the Ocean Floor

Preparation:
1. Prepare a model of the ocean floor. Form clay in the bottom of a plastic shoe box. Be sure to cover the sides of the box with paper or paint to prevent others from viewing the terrain.
2. Cut slits into the box lid or piece of cardboard. Be sure the slits are large enough for a ruler to slip through them.
3. Exchange models with another team of students.

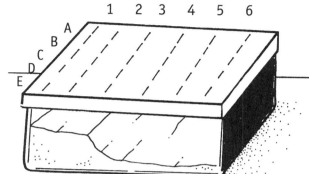

Procedure:
1. Begin at the first cut in the box top. Insert the ruler into the cut until it stops against something on the ocean floor. Do not force the ruler.
2. Plot the depth you recorded on the chart.
3. Continue doing this for each mark until you have recorded the depth at each mark.
4. When you have all of the points recorded, plot them on graph paper. When finished, connect them with a line. This will be a side profile of the ocean bottom.
5. Attempt to recognize features in your profile and label them on the graph. Draw a picture of the terrain:

Questions: *Answer the questions on the back of the paper.*
1. Label the parts of the ocean floor that you can recognize.
2. Describe what happens to the ocean floor as you move from left to right. Make sure you use terms that describe features on the floor such as slope, trench, etc.
3. Would this profile change if you moved left or right on your mapping expedition? Why or why not?

Ocean Floor Data Chart

	1	2	3	4	5	6
A						
B						
C						
D						
E						

ASTRONOMY

Fascinating Facts for Teachers

The Earth System

Earth scientists believe, based on observations of the earth itself and other objects in space, that the earth was born 4.5 billion years ago from a cloud of dust and gas floating in the Milky Way. Many of the space missions that have been undertaken have had exploration of the earth as their mission. Many of the satellites now in orbit have, as their primary mission, examination of the earth. Quite literally, the earth is the planet in our solar system about which we know most. We know the characteristics of the earth including the diameter (7,926 miles or 12,756 km at the equator), weight (6.6 sextillion tons or 6 sextillion metric tons), time it takes to complete a revolution (one day of 24 hours), and length of the year (one orbit of the sun in 365.25 days). We know it bulges slightly at the equator due to the centrifugal effect of its rotation, and that it probably has a molten center containing iron. We know that molten material carrying iron is capable of creating magnetic fields, and that is probably the reason the earth has a permanent magnetic field.

See Portal for Exploration "What Causes Day and Night"

See Portal for Exploration "The Foucault Pendulum"

We know a great deal about the motion of the earth in addition to its day and year. We know that the earth rotates on its axis to cause a day, revolves around the sun to cause a year, wobbles like a top as it rotates through the centuries, and that it is traveling through space with its companions, the other planets. The wobble in the axis of the earth is a very slow process taking thousands of years to complete. The wobble, however, is linked to periodic changes in climate which change over a very long time. Currently, the axis of the earth points, at one end, to a star we know as Polaris, or the North Star. Several thousands of years in the future, Polaris will not be the North Star as the "wobble" moves the orientation of the axis toward some other star.

We know the earth is a special planet—the only one where water exists in all three states in nature as water vapor, water, and ice. We know that the earth is the only planet on which life is confirmed to exist in any form. We know that about three-quarters of the earth's surface is covered with water, and the remainder is solid material. We know that the earth is surrounded by an atmosphere containing nitrogen and a lesser amount of oxygen, as well as small amounts of many other gasses. We also know that we must continue to explore the planet in order to find the resources that we use to maintain our life and our society.

EARTH'S GRAVITY

Gravity is a force that is explained only in terms of its effects rather than its actual cause. For some reason, objects tend to draw toward one another in direct proportion to their size, and they tend to loose attraction in proportion to the square of the distance that separates them. The formula that explains this phenomenon is given as:

$$G = \frac{m_1 m_2}{r^2}$$

This fancy formula just indicates that the greater the two masses involved actually are, the more gravity is exerted. This explains why your gravitational attraction to the earth is greater than your gravitational attraction to the wall closest to where you are sitting. You are drawn toward the center of the earth, causing a friction that far overcomes your gravitational attraction for the wall. Thus, you sit in a chair and do not go sliding into the nearest wall. This formula also explains why, even though the sun is very much larger than the earth, your gravitational attraction for the earth is greater because your distance to the earth (r) is smaller. As the distance increases, the gravitational attraction decreases quickly. Thus, you sit on your chair drawn to the center of the earth, and do not fly off of the earth's surface and fall into the sun.

See Portal for Exploration "Weightlessness"

When a force is exerted on you that resists gravity, that force causes you to have weight. The floor, for instance, exists between you and the center of earth's gravity. If you place a scale between you and the floor, the push you have against the scale is measured as your weight. However, if the floor were to vanish, you would begin to fall freely with respect to gravity, and the scale would read zero. This condition, the condition in which gravity acts freely on an object, is called weightlessness. Weightlessness is the condition in which astronauts exist as their space shuttle continually falls toward the earth (gravity is acting freely). While in orbit, the shuttle is moving so fast, that it constantly "overshoots" the earth. It is not that gravity is not present, it is simply that the velocity of the shuttle places it into an "orbit" around the center of gravity.

THE MOON

Our nearest neighbor in space is the moon. It is a body of rock about which we know a great deal due to the pioneering efforts of astronauts who visited there during a period beginning in 1969 and ending in 1972. However, there are many things that even the ancients knew. The moon orbits the earth in a regular pattern causing a repeating pattern of lunar appearance. We now know that the moon orbits roughly a quarter million miles from the earth and it has been known for quite some time that it takes 29½ days to complete the cycle from the appearance of one full moon to the next. However, the moon only takes 27⅓ days to complete an orbit of the earth and to rotate once on its axis, with respect to the stars. As a result of this odd timing and the changing angles presented by the orbit of the earth-moon system, the same face of the moon has been presented to the earth, probably, since the system began. It took the space program, both remote and manned exploration, to tell for sure what was on the hidden "back side" of the moon as well as the material of which the moon is made.

colored areas on the front side of the moon. These areas are highly cratered, rocky highlands, older in age than the dark material of the seas. The seas, aside from being younger than the light colored areas, are much more flat, and less cratered due to their younger age. The evidence is that the dark colored areas are eruptions of molten lava that have flooded vast portions of the lunar surface. These eruptions were probably due to the impact of particularly large objects that caused a vast amount of heat associated with the collision. The regions subsided and they became flooded with the erupted lava which, eventually, cooled into newer rock. Over time, the older, light colored areas have been continuously impacted and cratered. However, the front side of the moon, protected by the shadow of the earth, was not as heavily cratered, as the back, and the large impacts that caused the lava outbreaks have been hidden on the back side.

See Portal for Exploration "Phases of the Moon"

Half of the moon is lighted at all times by sunlight. However, residents of planet earth may not be able to see all of the reflected light, due to the geometry of the earth-moon system in relation to the sun. When the face of the moon that we see is completely lighted, we see that as a "full moon." When the face presented to the earth is directly opposite the lighted half of the moon, we see that as a "new moon." As the lighted face of the moon grows from new to full, the moon is said to be waxing; passing first from new to the waxing crescent, then to the first quarter, next to the waxing gibbous, and finally to the full moon. When the amount of the surface we see lighted is decreasing, the moon is said to be waning from full to waning gibbous, from third quarter to waning crescent, and finally back to new moon. These phases of the moon are repeated each month taking, as stated earlier, 29½ days.

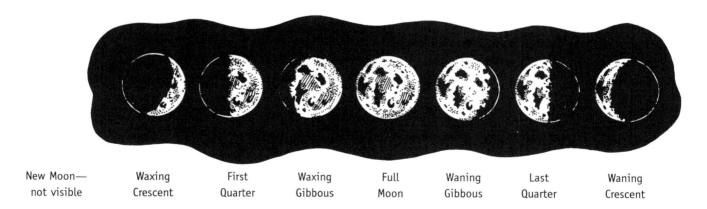

| New Moon— not visible | Waxing Crescent | First Quarter | Waxing Gibbous | Full Moon | Waning Gibbous | Last Quarter | Waning Crescent |

Phases of the Moon

The effect of the moon on the earth is pronounced. The most significant effect is gravity caused by the mass of the moon. The mass of the moon pulls on the earth and is the main cause of the twice daily tides experienced on the seas and oceans. While the moon pulls on the entire earth, the water that covers nearly three quarters of its surface is pulled more noticeably, causing a high area on the ocean and drawing water from the areas of the ocean in between. The areas from which water is drawn become the periods of low tides. It is widely believed that the moon effects people in a similar way. There are claims by police and hospital workers, and some teachers, that this phenomenon is true. In fact, the term "lunatic" derives from the belief that the moon affects human behavior. Logic suggests that this behavior anomaly may be true, but for reasons other than tidal effects. Perhaps the lack of moonlight stimulates criminal behavior, or perhaps students stay awake later on nights that the moonlight makes play in its many forms, more possible.

THE SUN

The sun is the center of the solar system, literally and figuratively. It is due to the unique placement of the earth's orbit, not too close yet not too far away, that allows life, as we know it, to exist on the earth. The sun is a very large object in relation to the earth. Its composition is mainly hydrogen and helium and traces of a great number of other elements. The sun generates it own energy in an atomic magic that happens deep within the sun due to its tremendous mass, and the associated gravity. Hydrogen is converted, in this process, directly into helium. The magic occurs when some of the mass in that reaction is "lost." This missing mass, called a mass defect by Albert Einstein, is converted directly to energy as a result of this fusion reaction and according to that famous equation, $E=mc^2$. Even a small mass defect (m in the equation), when multiplied by the huge constant c^2 (the speed of light, squared), results in a tremendous amount of energy (E in the equation). That energy constitutes the light and heat that bathes the earth and keeps us from freezing in the dark.

See Portal for Exploration "Eclipse in the Earth-Moon-Sun System"

The sun, earth, and moon have an interesting relationship that can be seen from time to time. The moon, although much smaller than the sun, is much closer to the earth. The unique relationship is that the distances and sizes involved make the sun and the moon appear to be the same size as viewed from the earth. The alignment of the sun, moon, and earth can cause some interesting phenomenon. During the period of the full moon, the shadow of the earth may be seen to fall upon the surface of the moon because the light from the sun cannot pass through the earth. This is called a lunar eclipse, named for what seems to be "blocked out." A lunar eclipse does not occur every month because the moon orbits the earth on an angular plane different than the plane on which the earth orbits the sun. From time to time, however, the angles present an alignment of the objects that can cause the lunar eclipse.

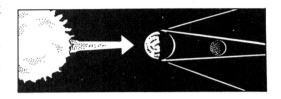

Another curious alignment can occur during the period of the full moon. When the planes of the orbits are exactly correct, the moon can project a shadow on the earth's surface as the moon passes between the sun and the earth. If one were to be in the shadow of the moon, the sun would appear to be "blocked out". This condition is called a solar eclipse and has been the source of a great deal of superstition. From the earth, the solar disk is intruded upon by a dark disk that, to the ancients, appeared to be a bite taken out of the sun. In a partial eclipse, the size of the darkened area grows and then decreases as the moon moves out of the line of sight. On very rare occasions, the moon moves into a position where, from the earth, the entire solar disk is darkened. On these occasions, daytime is truly turned into night. In scientific terms, this event presents a time when the corona, the outer regions of the sun, can be studied without the danger presented by the very bright, and blinding, photosphere.

Safety Concern: It is never safe to view the sun without appropriate viewing techniques. Direct viewing techniques involving filters are risky as a single crack or imperfection in the filter can cause permanent blindness. Indirect viewing techniques are safest to use. One such technique is shown here. Put a small hole (pinhole) in a piece of cardboard. Place a piece of white paper behind the cardboard so that the shadow of the cardboard falls on the paper. Move the cardboard toward and away from the white paper until an image is focused.

The surface of the sun, the photosphere, is seen through the eyes of solar observatories as a grainy surface of violent up and down drafts of bright, hot solar material. The fusion furnaces of the sun, located deep in the sun's interior, produce enough energy to boil the surface, much as the tops of clouds are boiled up by the uneven heating of the earth's surface. Occasionally, eruptions of solar material explode from the surface as flares and prominences, sending streams of solar materials into space. This material causes the solar wind as the particles can exert a small force against objects. More importantly, these particles stream into the earth's atmosphere causing interference with communications systems as well as the phenomenon known as the northern lights. Users of amateur radios are very familiar with the eleven year cycles of the solar storms that produce this interference. The solar storms are seen as dark splotches on an otherwise bright solar disk and have earned the name sunspots. Observing sunspots give us clues as to the rotation of the sun and show that the sun actually spins faster at its equator, giving more cause to understand the tortured nature of our nearest star.

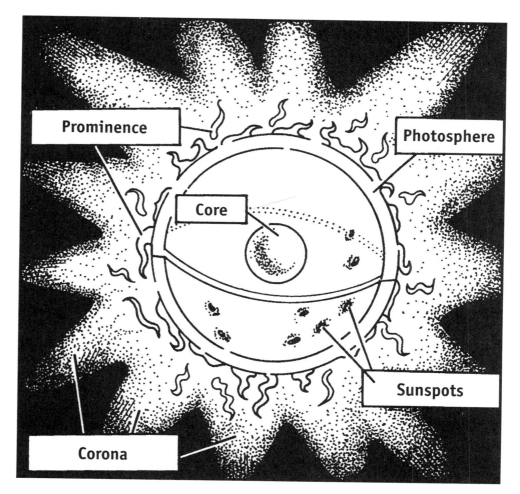

The Solar System

See Portal for Exploration "Physical Characteristics of the Planets"

INNER PLANETS

The planets of our solar system can be broken into two groups. The rocky inner planets are, in increasing distance from the sun, Mercury, Venus, Earth, and Mars. The planets are named for mythical characters based upon their appearance in the sky or their appearance in color. The rocky inner planets can be thought of as earth-sized, but are in actual terms, somewhat smaller than our home planet. Mercury, so close to the sun that its surface has a temperature that would melt lead, is small with no atmosphere. Any gasses that were close to its surface have been stripped by the close proximity of the sun and the intensity of the solar wind. It is named for the Roman winged messenger of the gods as it does have the shortest year, or time required for revolution around the sun. As the closest planet, it has the shortest circle to traverse. Venus, named for the goddess of beauty, is cloaked in a veil of gasses so thick and corrosive that its surface has been explored only by short lived remote systems killed by the attacking gasses. The surface of Venus is very hot as the incoming solar radiation is trapped by the heavy atmosphere creating the most intense greenhouse effect in the solar neighborhood.

The planet Mars, fourth from the sun and named for its red color and the Roman god of war, is the planet most like our own. It has a very light atmosphere, polar ice caps of water and carbon dioxide, and has been explored by remote vehicles. Much talk is heard regarding the launching of manned missions to Mars which would be reality mimicking literature. *The Martian Chronicles* speculate on the survival of a colony of astronaut-explorers on the Martian surface. Ever since Galileo observed lines on the Martian surface that he characterized as canals, the existence of civilizations on the Martian has tantalized humankind. However, Martian surface exploration has revealed no evidence of life on Mars in the form of any complex organic materials. Nevertheless, speculation regarding fossil evidence in rocky meteorites that are said to have originated from Mars has once again sparked the controversy as to whether earth remains the only planet hosting life.

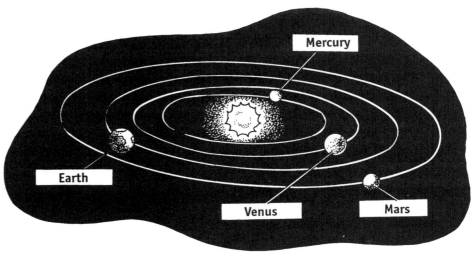

OUTER PLANETS

The outer planets are the gaseous giants. Jupiter, named for the Roman supreme deity, is the largest of the planets. It has a single storm on its surface known as the great red spot which is larger than the planet earth and has raged since observations of the planet were possible. It has a high rotation rate streaming its atmosphere into a horizontally striated image broken only by the great red spot. Although life, as we know it, at the surface would be impossible due to the high gravity of the planet, life on Jupiter's system of moons is the subject of much speculation and portrayed in the popular film, *2001: A Space Odyssey*. Saturn, named for the Roman god of agriculture, is well know for its complex ring system. Its size is second only to Jupiter. Uranus, third largest planet in the system is named for the Greek god of heaven and earth. Recent fly-bys of the Voyager spacecraft have proved that this planet also has a ring system, although smaller and less spectacular that the system of Saturn. It also has an anomaly in its rotation. Neptune is the eighth planet in the solar system, and fourth largest. Named for the god of the sea, it is the last of the gaseous giants. The ninth planet named for the god of the underworld, Pluto, was not discovered until 1930 and is very unusual. It revolves around the sun on a plane that is not aligned with the other planets, and the planet is a very small, rocky body. These characteristics, together with the elliptical nature of the orbit, lead astronomers to speculate that Pluto was a moon of Neptune, or is a visitor to this system caught by the sun's gravity as it moved from another system.

It is beyond the scope of this treatise to cover all of the interesting facts about the solar system. The purpose here is just to point out a few interesting facts, and to get the order of the planets right. A mnemonic device to remember the order is "**M**y **V**ery **E**xcellent **M**other **J**ust **S**ent **U**s **N**ine **P**ies:" Mercury, Venus, Earth, Mars, Jupiter, Saturn, Uranus, Neptune, and Pluto. The erratic orbit of Pluto does send the planet inside the orbit of Neptune for some small period of time during its year, but, on average, it is the most distant planet from the sun.

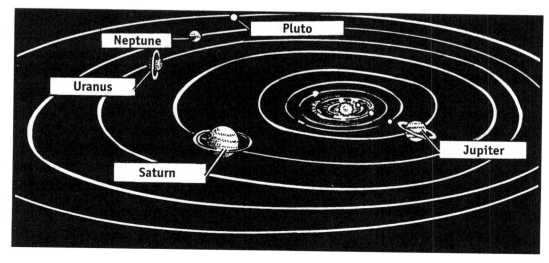

Other objects do exist in the solar system. They include comets, planetoids, and meteoroids. In a region between Mars and Jupiter, a large number of rock bodies, ranging in size from millimeters to several kilometers across, orbit the sun. This meteoroid belt may have originated as the orbit of a planet that failed to form during the formation of the solar system due to the enormous gravity of its close neighbor, Jupiter. Occasionally, a piece of this rock will enter the earth's atmosphere and burn up in a streak of light we know as a meteor. Rarely, a piece of this incoming rock will impact the earth. The resulting impact from a large meteorite can radically alter the physiography of the region and may alter the climate on a planetary level. A popular theory regarding the extinction of the dinosaurs is related to the impact of a particularly large meteorite. We know that such large impacts occur because several impact craters can be easily seen on a physiographic map of the world. One crater is in southern Africa, other craters clearly visible creating the Hudson Bay and the Gulf of Mexico, as well as hundreds of other, less obvious impacts.

See Portal for Exploration Impact Craters"

Another spectacular visitor to the solar system is the comet. Comets differ from meteors in that they rarely enter the atmosphere, give off a long-lasting light, and are more noticeable at times. Comets are large accumulations composed mostly of ice and some rock material. Their orbits are very elliptical taking, perhaps, thousands of years to visit the neighborhood of the earth before whipping around the sun to once again be thrown far away to disappear in the coldness of space. When the comet comes close to the sun, and the gasses begin to "melt" from the iceball, the gasses can be lit by the sun to appear, from the earth, as a beautiful, delta-shaped light in the sky. While it is visible, the comet does not appear to move fast as does a meteor, but its location in the sky does move from night to night. Although most people believe thath Haley's comet was most beautiful, the 1997 visit of comet Hale-Bopp provided a light show that was exceptional.

THE STARS

Legions of the Heavens

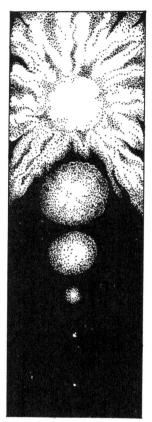

Stars are actually objects like our sun. They are large bodies in space that produce their own energy and glow brightly. Thousands of stars are visible from the earth, especially when viewing can be done from a place relatively free from both air pollution and light pollution. The stars are not all the same, and their sizes and temperatures vary widely. They do not all last the same amount of time, and all stars, eventually will burn out. As its hydrogen begins to run low, our star will swell to the point where its outermost layers will reach to the orbit of Mars. Although it will continue to produce energy, it will be distributed over a large area and the temperature will fall, making this a red giant. The red giant will eventually collapse into itself creating a very small, but intensely hot white dwarf. Eventually, as our sun runs out of its hydrogen fuel and begins to fuse helium into even heavier elements, it will run out of energy. The fusion furnace will die, and the sun will drift forever in space as a black dwarf.

Among the legions of the heavens, our sun is mediocre. The death of a star much larger than the sun would be much more violent. The star would swell into a red giant, but its collapse would generate a great deal more energy than our sun would be able to do. The outer layers of this star would be blasted away in a cataclysmic explosion called a nova. The largest stars would result in a super-nova. One of these explosions was noted in 1054 by the Chinese and the remnants of the star can be seen as the Crab Nebula. As the layers of gasses and heavy elements created in the explosion expand in space, they may become the copper in the wire in an electrical system, gold in your jewelry, and the carbon and oxygen that makes up a good percentage of your body. In that these heavier elements are only created in the cores of stars burning out, you can see that we are, in the truest sense, children of the stars.

See Portal for Exploration "Why Do Stars Twinkle"

As seen from the earth, the stars make up a set pattern in the sky. They are dependable and seem to us to be always were they were the minute, night, week, month, or year before. It is not the same with planets when they are visible. They are the wanderers across the backdrop of more permanent stellar patterns. Stars seems to twinkle as opposed to the planets, which do not. In order to learn where certain important stars were, patterns of stars were identified in the sky. These constellations were used in conjunction with familiar stories, Greek and Roman myths and Native American legends in order to teach their location and their meaning. The rising of a particular constellation may mean that it is time to plant, to harvest, or to get ready for winter. The stars can be used for navigation.

The North Star, Polaris, for example, is located in Ursa Minor, the Little Bear. If you can see the Little Bear, or recognize the Little Dipper, or use the pointer stars in the Big Dipper, you can find the North Star and, on a clear night, never be lost as to what direction north would be.

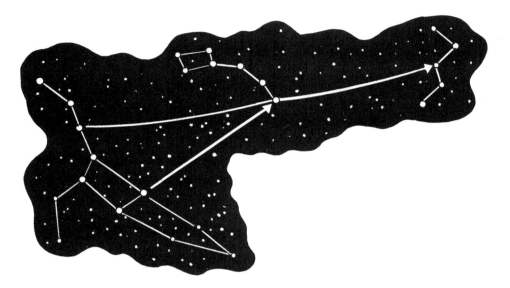

DEEP SPACE OBJECTS

Nebula are results of explosions of stars many times the mass of our own star, the sun. They may be light nebula that reflect the light produced by stars nearby, or dark clouds of gas that obscure the section of sky behind it. Nebula can be thought of as the birthplace of stars, because the gas in these clouds may condense into masses large enough to become stars of the future. The Pleiades, or Seven Sisters, is a very young star group still surrounded by the wisps of gas of the nebula from which they were born. The Pleiades is visible to the naked eye as a fuzzy patch in the constellation Taurus. If a pair of binoculars is used to look at that section of sky, the individual very young stars can be distinguished within the fuzzy region. This is but one example of a nebula and an associated star group.

Dying stars are the origin of many interesting phenomenon in the sky. The death of stars much larger than our own can result in the cataclysmic explosion creating a nova or supernova. What happens next is nothing short of amazing. The core of the star continues to burn, converting the last of the hydrogen fuel into helium, and then helium into heavier elements. At some point, the star begins to run out of fuel and the star becomes black. The star may be spinning very fast and only a small portion of the surface may still be emitting energy. As the star spins, the energy is made to flash like a light beacon, similar to a light house, but very fast. These pulsars are evidence that old stars are dying, much as nebula show that new stars are being born.

See Portal for Exploration "What Is a Million?"

The solar system exists in a galaxy consisting of a group of billions of stars shaped, more or less, as a pinwheel. Our galaxy is known as the Milky Way and is one of many in a group of galaxies. The Milky Way is 100,000 light years across, with a light year being the distance that light travels in one year, or 9.6 trillion kilometers. While our nearest stellar neighbor is 4.5 light years, the nearest galaxy, the Andromeda Galaxy, is two million light years away. Other galaxies are much more distant. Some galaxies are detectable only by the radiation they emit. Such distant galaxies are called quasars. The light and radiation they emit are changed due to a Doppler "red shift" which shows they are moving away from us, in all directions. This is evidence that our universe is expanding.

One of the most disturbing phenomenon in the universe is the black hole. These were merely theoretical objects in the recent past, but radiation sources observed by astronomers are thought to prove the existence of black holes. These objects are probably giant stars that have collapsed into tremendously massive small objects. Such a massive object would generate gravitational effects so large that not even light would be able to escape its pull. Evidence from astronomy exists in the form of radiation given off as objects begin to collide and disintegrate, spiraling into the gravity well of the black hole like water going down a drain. A black hole may even exist at the center of our own galaxy.

Space Exploration

See Portal for Exploration "Water Rockets"

The exploration of space has advanced our knowledge of the universe quickly. It is only three centuries ago that Galileo was restricted to his home for suggesting the sun, and not the earth, was the center of the solar system. Advances in technology associated with both optical and radio telescopes have extended our earthbound observation capabilities. But we have extended our observation beyond that. Rocketry, the reality of orbiting space telescopes, and the promise that space travel might hold, leads everyone to believe that space exploration will continue. In addition to the basic knowledge that is gained by such exploration, many spin-offs to the technology have changed our lives. The microcomputer, microwave technology, and communications systems are just a few examples of this spin-off technology. The form of this exploration, manned or unmanned, planetary or earth-centered, public or private, national or international, are all questions that are being addressed. But as history has shown, the human being must quest for the unknown and search for answers. Especially regarding space, the quest will continue.

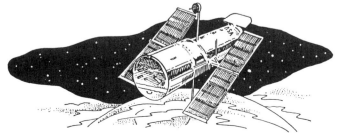

Asimov, I. *Great Space Mysteries*. Modern Publishing Company, 1988.
More of an encyclopedia, this book provides a great deal of factual information on deep space objects such as quasars, pulsars, black holes, and the formation of new stars.

Asimov, I. *Our Vast Home: The Milky Way and Other Galaxies*. Gareth Stevens, 1995.
This factual book incorporates theories and information about galaxies along with real photographs taken from space and telescopes. List of teacher references and contacts included.

Asimov, I. *The Birth of Our Universe*. Gareth Stevens, 1995.
A factual book that explains theories of how the universe began, it provides a great deal of information in a simplified form and gives practical examples that help explain these theories. List of teacher references and contacts are included.

Beach, L. *A Trip Around the Solar System*. Young Astronauts Council, 1987.
This *Young Astronaut's Book* takes the reader on a journey around the solar system. During the trip, the book describes each planet's unique characteristics. The book provides original photographs from NASA.

Bendick, J. *Space Travel*. Franklin Watts, 1982.
Suited for older students, this book describes the components of the universe including where space begins and what is considered part of our solar system. It also addresses the thought of space travel and space law as it provides information relating to space exploration.

Bendick, J. *The Universe: Think Big!* Millbrook Press, 1991.
This book answers many questions about our universe such as the components of the universe, how fast light moves, and how did the universe begin. The book provides vocabulary words in bold print and clear explanations.

Branley, F. M. *A Book of Stars for You*. Thomas Y. Crowell, 1967.
The *Let's-Read-and-Find-Out* book describes how people on earth can only see a small percentage of the stars in the universe. It explains the classes of stars such as white dwarfs, red giants, and the main sequence of stars based on size and temperature. Information relating to our sun as a star and constellations included.

Branley, F. M. *Comets*. Thomas Y. Crowell, 1984.
This *Let's-Read-and-Find-Out* book tells what comets are and how they are formed. It also provides their unusual orbits and gives special focus to Haley's comet.

Branley, F. M. *Eclipse: Darkness in Daytime*. Thomas Y. Crowell, 1973.
The *Let's-Read-and-Find-Out* book explains how eclipses occur, types of eclipses, and how to view eclipses. This book offers some dated information since it gives times and dates of eclipses that have already occurred.

Branley, F. M. *The Big Dipper*. Thomas Y. Crowell, 1962.
The *Let's-Read-and-Find-Out* book provides the reader with information on the Big Dipper during different seasons. It gives the names of the stars of the constellation and the origin of its name.

Branley, F. M. *What Makes Day and Night*. Thomas Y. Crowell, 1961.
This *Let's-Read-and-Find-Out* book explains how the earth rotates, causing the change from day to night in your local area.

Branley, F. M. *What the Moon Is Like*. Thomas Y. Crowell, 1986.
The *Let's-Read-and-Find-Out* book describes the characteristics of the moon. The book also discusses temperature variations on the light and darken sides, phenomena associated with decreased gravity such as being able to jump or hop long distances, and physical characteristics such as lunar seas and craters.

Cole, J. *The Magic School Bus Lost in the Solar System*. Scholastic, 1990.
A fictional account of Ms. Frizzle's class as they take a trip through the solar system

Conrad, P. *Call Me Ahnighito*. A Laura Geringer Book, 1995.
A fictional account of a true story that describes the finding of the meteorite Ahnighto in Greenland by Peary's expedition team, the story is told from the point of view of the meteorite as it describes its life here on earth.

Dorros, A. *Me and My Shadow*. Scholastic, 1990.
This book helps the reader investigate shadows. It also describes the position of the sun, moon, and earth for day and night.

Fields, A. *The Sun*. Franklin Watts, 1980.
Describes the characteristics of the sun's atmosphere, ability to produce heat and light, and solar activity such as sunspots, flares, and prominences. It also provides the reader with a description of the relationship between the sun, the earth, and the solar system.

Gibbons, G. *Stargazers*. Holiday House, 1992.
The factual story line describes the characteristics of stars and why they twinkle. Additionally, the book explains how constellations are named and provides diagrams of telescopes.

Hirst, R., & Hirst, S. *My Place in Space*. Orchard Books, 1988.
When Henry is asked if he knows where he lives, he describes his exact address from the street out through the universe. The book discusses components of the universe in size relationships.

Kandoian, E. *Under the Sun*. Dodd, Mead, and Company, 1987.
Molly's mother describes where the sun goes each night when she goes to sleep. The book is an aesthetic view of how the sun "rises and sets" due to the rotation of the earth.

Krupp, E. C. *The Big Dipper and You*. Morrow Junior Books, 1989.
This excellent book provides the reader with information about the Big Dipper. The book describes its movement, change in shape over time, and the folk lore associated with it and the North Star.

Lee, J. M. *Legend of the Milky Way*. Holt, Rinehart, & Winston, 1982.
The Chinese folktale describes the story of the Weaver Princess and a farm boy who fall in love and get married, but are forbidden to be together. The boundary that separates the two is said to be the Milky Way galaxy which in Chinese legend is referred to as the Silver River.

Leedy, L. *Postcards from Pluto*. Holiday House, 1993.
A group of children go on a tour of the solar system. As they encounter each planet or a celestial object, they send a postcard that describes its characteristics.

Maze, S. *I Want to Be an Astronaut*. Harcourt Brace, 1997.
This factual book describes what it is like to be an astronaut, the training to become an astronaut, and possible careers. It provides the reader with information through a series of short stories on each topic.

Moche, D. *What's Up There?* Scholastic, 1990.
This book answers individual questions such as "What makes the moon shine?" and "What is the sun made of?" for readers in an understandable manner by using clear explanations and diagrams.

Moore, P. *The Sun and Moon*. Copper Beech Books, 1994.
This book has vivid pictures that address topical questions. Topics include "how the sun moves," "sun spots," "the face of the moon," and "characteristics on the moon."

Oughton, J. *How the Stars Fell into the Sky*. Houghton Mifflin, 1992.
A Navajo folktale that describes a young woman's attempt to carefully place each star into a pattern in the sky. In the middle of her task, a coyote impatiently scatters the sky with the remaining stars. An excellent multicultural book that can be used for constellations.

Rockwell, A., & Brown, D. *Space Vehicles*. Dutton Children's Books, 1994.
Written at a very easy reading level, this book describes how satellites, space probes, and shuttles explore outer space.

Schwartz, D. M. *How Much is a Million?* Scholastic, 1985.
This book can aid the reader in understanding the concept of a million. Through various explanations and examples, the reader is introduced to a "million." A good book to use when talking about astronomical distances.

Simon, S. *Mercury*. Morrow Junior Books, 1992.
Provides the reader with known information relating to the planet Mercury. Most of this information was provided by the Mariner 10 probe.

Simon, S. *Jupiter*. Morrow Junior Books, 1985.
Provides the reader with known information relating to the planet Jupiter. It gives depictions and explanations of Jupiter's Giant Red Spot and four of the inner Galilean moons as seen from Voyager 1.

Simon, S. *Stars*. Morrow Junior Books, 1986.
Provides the reader with information about stars, their physical characteristics and composition. The book also describes the life cycle of a star as it is "born" and progresses through life to its "death." Additional information about stars, the Milky Way galaxy, and the study of stars is given.

Simon, S. *Venus*. Morrow Junior Books, 1992.
Provides the reader with known information about the planet Venus. It gives information relating to its climate and surface features that have been recently discovered.

Souza, D. M. *Northern Lights*. Carolrhoda, 1994.
A factual book that uses both real photographs and diagrams, the book explains what causes the auroras and their characteristics. Additional information is provided on the lore of the Northern Lights.

Trapani, I. *Twinkle, Twinkle Little Star*. Whispering Coyote Press, 1994.
A modern version of an old nursery rhyme, in the story a little girl is whisked away by the star she wishes on and is taken on a journey that explores the solar system and views the earth from above.

Verdet, J. P. *Earth, Sky, and Beyond: A Journey Through Space*. Lodestar Books, 1993.
This unique book takes the reader up through the earth's atmosphere into space, where it provides informative facts about each object: both natural, such as planets, asteroids, galaxies, and nebulas, and manufactured such as spaceships, probes, and satellites. Each page shows realistic art accompanied by scientific information.

Vogt, G. L. *Asteroids, Comets, and Meteors*. Millbook Press, 1996.
Provides the reader with information on asteroids, comets, and meteors. It gives information and actual photographs of meteorites that have struck the earth. Glossary included.

Vogt, G. L. *Uranus*. Millbook Press, 1993.
This factual book introduces the reader to the bluish-green planet Uranus. It provides the reader with information on its discovery, size, and surface features. Other books by the same author in this series include *Jupiter, Saturn,* and *Neptune*.

What Causes Day and Night?

Purpose:
- Explain how the rotation of the earth causes day and night by observing shadows.
- Describe the direction the earth rotates on its axis.

Materials Needed:

a long stick	clear sunny area
plastic discs or other markers	hammer
grease pencil	compass
colored pencils	paper

Introduction: The rotation of the earth on its axis results in the sun's rays striking the earth at different points and times. Because of this rotation, part of the earth at any given time is not receiving sunlight and part of it is, thus causing day and night to occur.

Procedure: See instructions on student lab sheet.

Behind the Scenes: The earth rotates in a counterclockwise motion or from west to east which causes objects in the sky to appear that they are moving from east to west. This explains why it appears that the sun rises in the east, moves across the sky, and sets in the west.

Answer Key For Questions:
1. Answers will vary. For example, the shadow will move to the east.
2. Answers will vary. For example, the shortest shadow is visible at mid-day and lengthens during earlier and later times. The shadow's length changes as the sun appears to move across the sky.
3. Answers will vary. For example, rotation is toward the east.

Literature Links: Branley, F. M. *What Makes Day and Night*. Thomas Y. Crowell, 1961.
Dorros, A. *Me and My Shadow*. Scholastic, 1990.
Kandoian, E. *Under the Sun*. Dodd, Mead, and Company, 1987.

Portals for Expansion:

Math
- Create a graph that represents the times of sunrise and sunset each day. Have students observe and compare the results over a period of time.
- Using information on time zones, have students determine the time in other parts of the world.

Language Arts
- Read *Under the Sun* by E. Kandoian and have the students predict the ending of the story.
- Ask students to write their own versions of where the sun goes and the adventures it has when they sleep at night.

Art
- Trace students' shadows on the playground with chalk at different times of the day. Discuss why shadows get "longer" and "shorter" depending on where the sun is in the sky.
- Have a shadow show using hand puppets. Try to make the shadows grow and shrink by changing the way the light hits them.

Social Studies
- List ten major cities in the world. Determine the time zone for each city. Have students write a report on these cities comparing activities that may occur simultaneously.

What Causes Day and Night?

Setup:
1. Hammer the stick into the ground so that it will stand upright and perpendicular to the ground.
2. Using your compass, determine north. Place a marker with an "N" on it on the north side of the stick.
3. Mark the other three cardinal points with plastic discs that have been labeled—S, E, and W.
4. The stick will cast a shadow on the ground somewhere. Mark the end point of the shadow with a plastic disc or other marker. Write the time on the marker with a grease pencil.

Procedure:
1. On a sheet of paper, make a chart that shows the compass directions. See the diagram.

2. Using a black crayon or colored pencil, draw on your chart where the stick's shadow is cast on the ground. Label the time.
3. Where will the shadow be cast after ten minutes? Using a red pencil or crayon, draw your prediction and label it on your chart.
4. After ten minutes, observe where the shadow is located. Place a marker at the tip of the stick's shadow. Using the grease pencil, write the time on the marker. On your chart, use a blue pencil or crayon to draw the position of the shadow and label its time.
5. Continue to observe the shadow at various times. After markers have been placed on the ground throughout the day, record your observations on the chart.

Questions: *Answer the questions on the back of the paper.*
1. Toward which direction did you predict the stick's shadow would move? Which direction did it move? Based on this prediction and observation, describe the direction the shadow will move for the rest of the day. Explain your answer.
2. Describe what you notice about the length of the stick's shadow and the time the shadow was cast. When is the shadow the shortest? the longest? Why does the shadow's length change?
3. Based on your observations, describe what direction the earth rotates and your reason.

Foucault Pendulum

Teacher Demonstration

Purpose:
- Explain how the motion of the Foucault pendulum shows that the earth is rotating by making observations.

Materials Needed:
model of the Foucault pendulum
dominoes
turntable or furniture swivel

Procedure:
1. Place the model of the Foucault pendulum on a turntable.
2. Start the pendulum swinging.
3. Show that the pendulum swings in the same direction due to momentum by allowing the swinging pendulum to slow and stop without moving the turntable.
4. Set up several dominoes on either side of the pathway of the pendulum.
5. Explain that the turntable will rotate as the earth rotates on its axis.
6. Begin the swinging of the pendulum and very slowly rotate the turntable until all dominoes are knocked down.
7. Ask the students if the direction of the pendulum changed as the turntable rotated.
8. Ask the students what is proved by the apparent change in direction of the Foucault pendulum hanging in many science centers across the nation.

Behind the Scenes:
Preparation of the Foucault pendulum model: Bend a 2-foot (61 cm) long, ¼-inch (7 mm) diameter threaded rod into a horseshoe shape. Cut a 9-inch (23 cm) diameter circular piece of plywood and drill two ¼-inch (7 mm) holes near the outside of the circle on opposite ends of a diameter. Secure the ends of the threaded rod into the circular piece of plywood using a ¼-inch (7 mm) nut countersunk so that they do not protrude from the plywood. Suspend a line with a weight from the top of the horseshoe.

Literature Links:
Branley, F. M. *What Makes Day and Night?* Thomas Y. Crowell, 1961.
Kandoian, E. *Under the Sun.* Dodd, Mead, and Company, 1987.

Portals for Expansion:

Social Studies
- Research stories from other cultures that explain why the sun rises and sets.

Language Arts
- Write a story that gives a novel or unique explanation for what happens to the sun at night.
- Write letters to local or national science centers asking them for information regarding the sizes, construction, etc. of their pendulums. Compare and contrast this information.

Science
- Visit a nearby science center to make observations of a Foucault pendulum when you arrive and when you leave.

Math
- Determine how many swings will occur during the time it takes the pendulum to rotate once on the turntable.

Weightlessness
Teacher Demonstration

Purpose:
- Observe momentary weightlessness in different objects.
- Describe where weightlessness occurs and the reasons.

Materials Needed:

Demonstration 1:
Styrofoam cup
pointed object
water
bucket or basin

Demonstration 2:
heavy book
bathroom scale
foam mattress

Demonstration 3:
clear tube
colored water
caps for tube ends
silicone seal

Introduction: When orbiting the earth, spacecraft experience a condition described as weightlessness. The spacecraft is in a state of free fall as it orbits. Objects and people on board who are not tied down also experience weightlessness and are in the same state of free fall. Some amusement park rides achieve the experience of weightlessness for a second or two.

Procedure:

Demonstration 1: A Styrofoam Cup Demonstrates Weightlessness
1. Punch a small hole in the side of the cup near its bottom.
2. Hold your thumb over the hole. Fill the cup with water while holding it directly over the basin which rests on the floor.
3. Have students write down their predictions to the following question: *What do you think will happen if I remove my thumb?*
4. Remove your thumb and allow some water to stream out of the cup and into the basin. Students should record their observations.
5. Reseal the hole with your thumb and refill the cup.
6. Ask your students to write down their predictions to the following question: *Will water stream out of the hole if I drop the cup?*
7. Drop the filled cup into the basin. The demonstration is more effective if you hold the cup as high as possible before dropping it. Students should record their observations.

Demonstration 2: Books and Bathroom Scales
1. Place a heavy book on a bathroom scale as you hold both in the air.
2. Ask students to record the weight of the book.
3. Have students write down their predictions to the following question: *What do you think will happen to the weight of the book if I drop both the scale and book together?*
4. Drop the book and the scale together from a height of about 2 meters onto a foam mattress or some pillows.
5. As it drops, quickly observe the book's weight.

Demonstration 3: Air Bubbles

1. Obtain a clear plastic tube with PVC threaded plugs for caps.
2. Cap one end and seal it with silicone sealant.
3. Fill the tube with colored water and cap the other end.
4. A small amount of air in the tube will form a bubble.
5. Have students write down their predictions to the following question: *What do you think will happen to the bubble if I turn this tube upside down?*
6. Turn the tube upside down and allow the bubble to rise to the top.
7. Encourage students to write down their predictions to the following question: *What do you think will happen to the bubble if I turn this tube upside down and toss the tube to someone across the room?*
8. Turn the tube upside down, allowing the bubble to begin to rise to the top. Have someone quickly observe where the bubble is and then toss it to someone across the room trying to keep the tube perpendicular to the ground.
9. Have a student observe where the bubble is when the tube is caught by the other person.

Behind the Scenes:

Demonstration 1: The falling cup, for a moment, demonstrates weightlessness. When the cup is stationary, the water freely pours out of the cup. As the cup falls, the water remains inside the cup for its entire fall.

Demonstration 2: As the book and scale drop, the book's weight becomes zero for a moment.

Demonstration 3: As the tube is tossed through the air, the bubble stops rising to the top.

Literature Links:

Bendick, J. *Space Travel.* Franklin Watts, 1982.
Branley, F. M. *What the Moon Is Like.* Thomas Y. Crowell, 1986.
Cole, J. *The Magic School Bus Lost in the Solar System.* Scholastic, 1990.
Maze, S. *I Want to Be an Astronaut.* Harcourt, Brace, 1997.

Portals for Expansion:

Language Arts
• Have students write a story or poem describing how it would feel to experience weightlessness in space. Have the students give descriptive examples of how they would move, eat, do homework, etc.

Math
• Look up the gravitational constants for the other planets. For example, on the Moon a person would weigh one-sixth of what he/she weighs on Earth because there is a smaller gravitational pull. Calculate what your weight would be on the other planets.

Weightlessness Demonstrations

Questions: *Answer the following questions. If necessary, record your observations on the back of the paper.*

Demonstration #1:

1. **Predict:** What do you think will happen if the thumb is removed from the hole?

2. **Record** your observations of what actually happened. Use diagrams if necessary.

3. **Predict:** Will water stream out of the hole if the cup is dropped?

4. **Record** your observations of what actually happened.

Demonstration #2:

1. **Record** the weight of the book while it is held. _____

2. **Predict:** What do you think will happen to the weight of the book if both the scale and book are dropped together?

3. **Record** your observations of what actually happened.

Demonstration #3:

1. **Predict:** What do you think will happen to the bubble if the tube is turned upside down?

2. **Record** your observations of what actually happened. Use diagrams if necessary.

3. **Predict:** What do you think will happen to the bubble if the tube is turned upside down and then tossed to someone across the room?

4. **Record** what happened when the tube was tossed across the room.

Phases of the Moon

Teacher Demonstration

Purpose:
- Describe the phases of the moon.
- Explain how the phases of the moon occur.

Materials Needed:
volleyball
spotlight
signs for the phases of the moon
white paint

Introduction: The phases of the moon are the daily changes in the moon's appearance as it is viewed from the earth. The moon's phases occur for two reasons. First, the moon is visible only because it reflects sunlight. Second, it revolves around the earth in orbit. Depending on the moon's position in relation to the earth, people may see only part of the side which is reflecting the sun's light. During a full moon, the entire side can be viewed from earth. During the new moon phase, the side reflecting the sun's light is not visible on earth.

Procedure:
1. Paint the volleyball bright white with the paint. This represents the moon.
2. Place a spotlight against or mounted to the wall of one side of the room. The spotlight represents the "sun."
3. Choose students to hold signs that represent the phases of the moon. Using the diagram, position the students in their proper locations.
4. Follow the instructions on the student lab sheet.

Behind the Scenes: An explanation of why we only see part of the surface that is reflecting light will be needed to help the students understand. At any given point, half of the moon is reflecting the sun's light. If the earth's shadow should fall on the side of the moon which is reflecting light an eclipse occurs. It takes a period of 27 1/3 days for the moon to make one complete revolution around the earth. A Blue Moon occurs when there are two full moons in the same calendar month.

Answer Key For Questions:
1. Answers will vary. For example, the phases are caused by the relative positions of the earth and moon in reference to the sun.
2. A lunar eclipse
3. Answers will vary. For example: Yes. The phases occur once each month.

Literature Links:
Branley, F. M. *Eclipse: Darkness in Daytime.* Thomas Y. Crowell, 1973.
Branley, F. M. *What the Moon Is Like.* Thomas Y. Crowell, 1986.
Cole, J. *The Magic School Bus Lost in the Solar System.* Scholastic, 1990.
Dorros, A. *Me and My Shadow.* Scholastic, 1990.
Moche, D. *What's Up There?* Scholastic, 1990.
Moore, P. *The Sun and Moon.* Copper Beech, 1994.

Portals for Expansion:

Math

- Have the students chart how many days the moon is seen in each of its phases progressing from "new moon" to "full moon."
- Chart what time the "moonrise" is each day. This information can be obtained from the daily newspaper and should change daily.

Social Studies

- Read old stories relating to the changing of the moon and superstitions associated with each phase. A good area to investigate is Native American literature, Chinese proverbs, and Greek and Roman beliefs.
- Encourage students to design their own names for the moon. For example, the "Harvest Moon" is the October moon for Native Americans. Have students explain their reasoning for each name.

Language Arts

- Write "ghost stories" of what happens during a full moon. Students may create books that are complete with illustrations, title pages, and stories for inclusion in the classroom library.

Science

- Track the high and low tides around the full moon and new moon times. Chart what happens to the water level during the different phases of the moon.
- Give the students a calendar and have them sketch the moon during an entire cycle. Students also can track additional information relating to the times the moon is visible.
- Using binoculars, observe the moon at night. Refer to a field guide to identify land features.

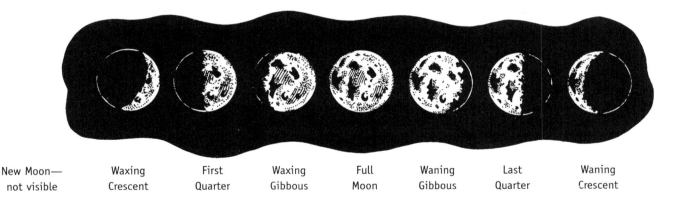

| New Moon— not visible | Waxing Crescent | First Quarter | Waxing Gibbous | Full Moon | Waning Gibbous | Last Quarter | Waning Crescent |

Phases of the Moon

Phases of the Moon

Procedure:
1. Dim the lights in the room.
2. The students sit in the center of the room. They represent "earth."
3. One person holds the ball which represents the "moon." This person begins the demonstration by standing between the "earth" and the "sun." This position is called "new moon." Have the students observe how much of the moon's surface is reflecting light.
4. The person holding the ball continues to move in a counterclockwise motion around "earth" stopping at each position, allowing students time to complete the chart below.

Observation: Complete the diagram to show the phases of the moon you saw in the demonstration.

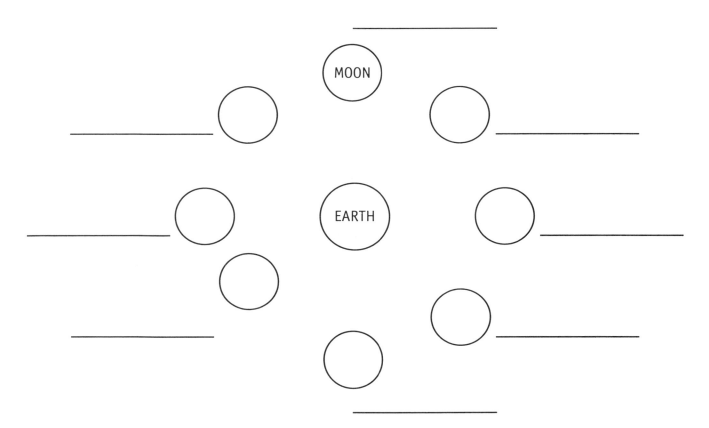

Questions: *Answer questions on the back of the paper.*
1. Describe why we observe different phases of the moon.
2. What occurs when the moon passes through the earth's shadow?
3. Do we ever see a "new moon"? Why or why not?

Eclipses in the Earth-Moon-Sun System

Teacher Demonstration

Purpose:
- Explain the difference between solar and lunar eclipses by explaining what object is blocked by what other object.
- Explain when eclipses will happen by drawing diagrams of the relative positions of the sun, earth, and the moon.

Materials Needed:
large globe desk light
planet earth globe
softball to represent the moon

Procedure:
1. Turn on the desk lamp and turn off the classroom lights.
2. Hold the globe and the softball so that the light from the globe illuminates half of each, possibly by placing them alongside each other.
3. Draw a diagram, as viewed from the top, of the earth and how it is lighted by the globe lamp.
4. Move the softball moon in a circle around the globe of the earth. When the softball moon is behind the earth, make sure the softball moon is above the level of the earth.
5. Draw, as viewed from the globe of the earth, the face of the moon that is lighted by the desk lamp. Label this phase of the moon.
6. Move the softball moon in its orbit around the globe of the earth until it is between the earth and the sun, but a little lower than the earth.
7. Draw, as viewed from the globe of the earth, the face of the moon that is lighted by the desk lamp. Label this phase of the moon.
8. Now draw, from the perspective of the globe of the earth, the face of the softball moon as it approaches, goes directly behind, and then emerges from the shadow of the globe of the earth. (*Lunar eclipse is demonstrated.*)
9. Label this as an eclipse of the moon since it is the light of the moon being blocked out.
10. Now draw the path of the shadow projected by the moon as it crosses directly in front of the globe of the earth. (*Solar eclipse is demonstrated.*)

Literature Links:
Branley, F. M. *Eclipse: Darkness in Daytime*. Thomas Y. Crowell, 1973.
Branley, F. M. *What the Moon Is Like*. Thomas Y. Crowell, 1986.
Dorros, A. *Me and My Shadow*. Scholastic, 1990.
Fields, A. *The Sun*. Franklin Watts, 1980.
Moore, P. *The Sun and Moon*. Copper Beech, 1994.

Portals for Expansion:

Social Studies
- Explore the myths and legends behind solar and lunar eclipses.

Language Arts
- Write a poem or story about how you believe an ancient civilization may have reacted to an eclipse.
- Write a script for a television or radio announcer who follows an eclipse from start to finish.

Science
- Find out when the next lunar and solar eclipses that are visible in your local area will occur. If needed, contact a local observatory or planetarium.

Eclipses in the Earth-Moon-Sun System

Procedure:

1. Turn on the lamp. Turn off the classroom lights. Draw, viewed from the top, how the globe of the earth and the softball moon look.

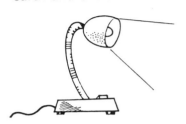

MOON

EARTH

2. Hold the softball moon behind the earth, but not in its shadow. Color the face of the moon.
What phase is this? _____

MOON

3. Hold the softball moon in front of and a little below the earth. Color the face of the moon.
What phase is this? _____

MOON

4. Draw the face of the softball moon as it approaches (A), goes directly behind (B), and emerges (C) from the shadow of the globe.

   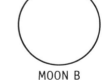   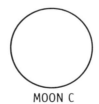

MOON A   MOON B   MOON C

What kind of eclipse is this? _____

5. Draw the path of the shadow projected by the moon as it crosses directly in front of the globe of the earth.

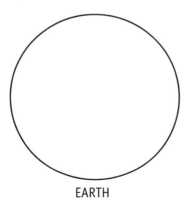

What kind of eclipse is this? _____

EARTH

Physical Characteristics of the Planets

Purpose:
- Describe the distances of the planets from the sun.
- Explain differences between the inner planets and the outer planets.
- Demonstrate that it will take longer for an outer planet to orbit the sun than it does for an inner planet to orbit the sun.

Materials Needed:
playground area
sidewalk chalk
measuring tape
string
stopwatch

Introduction: Each planet in our solar system has unique characteristics. For example, Saturn is well known for having a massive set of rings made of ice and debris. However, did you also know that Jupiter and Uranus have a series of rings? This activity will explain one major characteristic of the planets and allow for the exploration of the others through books.

Preparation:
1. Using the chart provided, develop a scale version of the distance from the sun for each planet. A scale version is provided for you, but you also may develop your own.
2. Select a point for the sun somewhere in the center of the playground. Using sidewalk chalk, draw a picture of the sun.
3. Using the scale version of the distance from the sun to Mercury, measure the distance and draw Mercury.
4. Draw a partial orbit for Mercury around the sun. A good way of constructing an arc for the partial orbit is to have a student stand in the center of the sun with a long piece of string which reaches to Mercury. Have a second student hold that string and using the chalk, draw the arc for the partial orbit around the sun.
5. Continue the process of measuring a planet's distance from the sun and then drawing a partial arc for its orbit, until each planet is represented on the playground.
6. Follow Step 4 for making each arc. By doing this, each orbit will be as circular as possible. You should inform the students that this is actually incorrect because the planets' orbits are elliptical.

Procedure:
1. After your solar system is complete, begin with the orbit of Mercury and have each student walk along the orbit for one minute by placing one foot directly in front of the other in a toe to heel fashion.
2. Observe how far the students are able to move around the sun.
3. Repeat Steps 1 and 2 with each planet's orbit.

Behind the Scenes: As children walk along the orbit of each planet, they will observe a relationship between the planet's distance from the sun and the size of its orbit. Be sure to explain to the students that at some point in Pluto's orbit around the sun, it actually moves inside of Neptune's orbit.

Answer Key For Questions:
1. Answers may vary. For example, the outer planets are much more distant from the sun.
2. Answers may vary. For example, the distance increased greatly.
3. The distance from the sun is so great.
4. Answers may vary. For example, the year is much longer.

Literature Links:
Asimov, I. *The Birth of Our Universe*. Gareth Stevens, 1995.
Beach, L. *A Trip Around the Solar System*. The Young Astronauts Council, 1987.
Cole, J. *The Magic School Bus Lost in the Solar System*. Scholastic, 1990.
Leedy, L. *Postcards from Pluto*. Holiday House, 1993.
Simon, S. *Mercury*. Morrow Junior Books, 1992.
Simon, S. *Jupiter*. Morrow Junior Books, 1985.
Simon, S. *Venus*. Morrow Junior Books, 1992.
Verdet, J. P. *Earth, Sky, and Beyond: A Journey Through Space*. Lodestar Books, 1993.
Vogt, G. L. *Uranus*. Millbook Press, 1993.

Portals for Expansion:

Math
- Develop different scale distances for the planets and redo this activity.
- Look up how many days it takes each planet to orbit the sun to determine its "year." Have students figure out how old they would be on each planet. Ask them to explain if they would be older or younger than they are now on each planet.
- Continue this activity in a very large area and have the students determine how many steps it would take to actually orbit the "sun" as a particular planet and the time required. Compare those numbers to actual data.

Language Arts
- Have students write riddles or puzzles about the planets based on factual information. Allow other students to try to solve the riddles.
- Have students write Haiku about each planet, describing the conditions on the planet, the planet's weather, or other nature-related items.

Art
- Using a smaller scale, design and draw a mural of the solar system on the wall in a long hallway. Have students paint in identifiable characteristics on each planet.

Social Studies
- Have students read about the planets and identify in which age each was discovered. For example, the inner planets were known during the time of the Ancients and were referred to as the "wanderers."

Physical Characteristics of the Planets

Procedure: How far around the sun can you walk in one minute in each planet's orbit? Compare the distances.

Planet	Average Distance to Sun (Millions of Kilometers)	Scale Distance (Meters)	Your Scale Distance
Mercury	58	.55	
Venus	108	1.02	
Earth	150	1.42	
Mars	228	2.17	
Jupiter	778	7.37	
Saturn	1429	13.51	
Uranus	2875	27.30	
Neptune	4504	42.61	
Pluto	5900	55.91	

Questions: *Answer the questions on the back of the paper.*
1. What did you notice about the distances of the inner planets from the sun compared to the outer planets' distances from the sun?
2. Describe what happened to the distance you traveled around the sun on each planet's orbit as you got further away from the sun.
3. Why do you think it takes a longer period of time for Pluto and Neptune to travel around the sun than it does for Mercury?
4. If it takes longer for the outer planets to travel around the sun, what happened to the length of each planet's year? Explain your answer.

What Is a Million?

Purpose: • Perform a serial dilution of food coloring, demonstrating concentrations from 1 in 10 to 1 in 100 billion using a eyedropper and spot plate.

Materials Needed: **For student group:**
spot plate
eyedropper
240 mL (1 cup) of water
vial of food coloring
paper towels

Introduction: A good way to introduce the topic of "a million" is to begin by reading *What Is a Million?* by D. M. Schwartz. This book actually uses stars on its pages to explain the concept of a million.

Procedure: 1. Number the spots on the plate horizontally from 1 to 12. See page 167.
2. See the student lab sheet for further instructions.
3. Answers for the serial dilution: Spot 1: 1 in 10, Spot 2: 1 in 100, Spot 3: 1 in 1,000, Spot 4: 1 in 10,000, Spot 5: 1 in 100,000, Spot 6: 1 in 1 million, Spot 7: 1 in 10 million, Spot 8: 1 in 100 million, Spot 9: 1 in 1 billion, Spot 10: 1 in 10 billion, Spot 11: 1 in 100 billion, Spot 12: 1 in 1 trillion.

Behind the Scenes: The concept of "What is a million?" is difficult to explain to students since odds are they have never seen a million of anything. This activity can assist you in showing that although there may be millions of stars in the galaxy, using just the naked eye prevents you from seeing most of them. You can assist the students in understanding this concept using a variety of adaptations. For example, there are nine planets and our sun, forming the solar system which is part of the Milky Way Galaxy; with the naked eye, you can see some of planets. They are at least visible, just like the concentration of the first spot plate which is 1 in 10.

Answer Key For Questions: 1. Answers will vary. For example, the color cannot be seen in Spot 5 (1 in 100 thousand).
2. Answers will vary. For example, one in a million is great visual acuity.

Literature Links: Bendick, J. *The Universe: Think Big!* Millbrook Press, 1991.
Gibbons, G. *Stargazers*. Holiday House, 1992.
Lee, J. M. *Legend of the Milky Way*. Holt, Rinehart, & Winston, 1982.
Oughton, J. *How the Stars Fell into the Sky*. Houghton Mifflin, 1992.
Schwartz, D. M. *How Much Is a Million?* Scholastic, 1985.
Simon, S. *Stars*. Morrow Junior Books, 1986.

Portals for Expansion: **Math**
• Using the story of a needle in a haystack, discuss why the color disappeared around Spot 5.
• Begin collecting some type of small item. Graph the number collected each day and then determine the average number collected per week. Calculate how long it would take your class to collect a million of these items.
Social Studies
• Using an atlas, determine which cities in the world have over a million people living in them and mark them on a world map. Discuss the pattern that develops.

What Is a Million?

Procedure:

1. In Spot 1, place one drop of food coloring from the vial and nine drops of water using the clean eyedropper.

   Ratio of "Drops of Coloring" per "Total Drops" is _____ of _____.

Record.

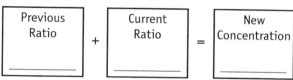

Drops of Food Coloring		Drops of Water		Total Drops
_____	+	_____	=	_____

2. In Spot 2, transfer one drop from Spot 1. Add nine drops of clean water. The dilution is now reduced by a factor of 1/10 (one drop in a total of ten) making a new concentration. *Note:* To calculate the new concentration, multiply the previous concentration (1/10 in this case) by the dilution (1/10).

Record.

Previous Ratio		Current Ratio		New Concentration
_____	+	_____	=	_____

3. In each of the other spots, place nine drops of clean water. Starting at Spot 3, transfer one drop of water from Spot 2. Continue in the same manner for all spots.

4. Complete the chart. Using a crayon or colored pencil, shade in the darkness of the color you observe in your spot plate.

1. ◯ dilution:_____

2. ◯ dilution:_____

3. ◯ dilution:_____

4. ◯ dilution:_____

5. ◯ dilution:_____

6. ◯ dilution:_____

7. ◯ dilution:_____

8. ◯ dilution:_____

9. ◯ dilution:_____

10. ◯ dilution:_____

11. ◯ dilution:_____

12. ◯ dilution:_____

Questions:

1. Where did you begin to not be able to see the color anymore?
2. Based on this activity, do you think that you can see "a million" stars in the sky? Why or why not?

Impact Craters

Purpose:
- Demonstrate how meteorites cause impact craters on the surface of the earth, moon, and other planets.
- Explain how the diameter of the meteorite affects the size of the crater made.
- Describe how the speed of the meteorite affects the size of the crater made.

Materials Needed:

large box or sand table   sand
ruler   tape measure
round objects in various sizes and weights   balance
ladder or stepping stool

Introduction: Craters are found in almost every geographic region. Most of these craters were formed when meteorites struck the earth. The width and depth of a crater depends on the speed and size of the meteorite when it strikes the ground.

Procedure:
1. Place the box on a flat, level surface and fill with 10–15 cm of sand.
2. See the student lab sheet for further instructions.

Behind the Scenes: Scientists believe that the surfaces on the moon and Mercury were scarred by craters over time. However, since there is no erosion on the moon's surface, as well as no forces to rebuild the moon, these craters remained. The earth's surface has also been scarred from meteorite impacts; however, due to erosion, rebuilding forces (volcanic activity), and continental plates movement, most of the earth's craters have been filled in with sediments or destroyed.

Answer Key For Questions:
1. Answers will vary. For example, the craters became larger or smaller in size.
2. Answers will vary. For example, the craters became deeper. Yes. The velocity will increase if the object is dropped from a higher point.
3. Answers will vary. For example, the moon's surface has been scarred by many impact craters.

Literature Links:
Branley, F. M. *What the Moon Is Like*. Thomas Y. Crowell, 1986.
Moore, P. *The Sun and Moon*. Copper Beech, 1994.
Simon, S. *Mercury*. Morrow Junior Books, 1992.
Vogt, G. L. *Asteroids, Comets, and Meteors*. Millbook Press, 1996.

Portals for Expansion:

Language Arts
- Write a story from the perspective of a news reporter or broadcaster who is expecting a meteorite to hit the earth. Interview other students and family members for the story.
- Using the same idea of a meteorite hitting the earth, have the students write a narrative story or poem describing life during the time of the dinosaurs.

Math
- Calculate the average speed at which each "meteorite" was falling by dividing the total distance traveled by the amount of time. Compare crater sizes when a fast meteorite hits the "earth" compared to a slower meteorite.

Art
- Create "meteorite art" allowing students to drop round-shaped sponges soaked with paint onto large sheets of butcher paper.
- Create imaginary creatures that might live in craters on other planets or the moon. Construct the creatures using scrap craft materials.

LAB
Astronomy

Impact Craters

Procedure:
1. Measure the diameter of one of the balls and its mass. Record them on the chart.
2. Using a small ladder or stepping stool, have a student climb to the top of the ladder and drop the ball into the sand box. When the ball hits the sand, it will cause an impact crater to form.
3. Carefully remove the ball from the sand box and measure the diameter of the crater. Record it on the chart.
4. Using the ruler, carefully measure the depth of the crater by placing the ruler into the deepest point vertically. Lay a sheet of paper onto the sand, then determine the crater's depth by reading the ruler. Record the measurment. Smooth out the sand.
5. Repeat this activity with several different spherical objects that have different diameters and weights. Record each trial on the chart.

Diameter of Ball and Description	Mass of Ball	Diameter of Crater	Depth of Crater

Questions: *Answer the questions on the back of the paper.*
1. Describe what happened to the diameter of the impact crater when you used different-sized objects.
2. What happened to the depth of your crater when you dropped objects with more mass? Do you think it would make a difference if you dropped them from a higher point? Why or why not?
3. Describe the moon's surface and hypothesize why it looks like this.

Why Do Stars Twinkle?

Purpose: • List some factors that create the twinkling effect of stars.

Materials Needed:
candle
"dirty" chalkboard eraser
flashlight
red filter or red cellophane
blue filter or blue cellophane

Introduction: Observatories are often located in remote and high areas so that the effects of air pollution, heat pollution of the air, and light pollution does not distract from the observation. This lab activity attempts to demonstrate the negative effects of each of these types of pollution on the quality of different kinds of light that can be observed coming from a flashlight. Students should begin to observe that not all wavelengths of light are affected by pollution to the same degree.

Procedure: See instructions on student lab sheet.

Answer Key For Questions:
1. Answers will vary. For example, the entire sky can be viewed.
2. Answers will vary. For example, the remote area is darker than an urban area because there is less light pollution.

Literature Links:
Asimov, I. *Great Space Mysteries*. Modern Publishing Company, 1988.
Gibbons, G. *Stargazers*. Holiday House, 1992.
Krupp, E. C. *The Big Dipper and You*. Morrow Junior Books, 1989.
Lee, J. M. *Legend of the Milky Way*. Holt, Rinehart, & Winston, 1982.
Moche, D. *What's Up There?* Scholastic, 1990.
Oughton, J. *How the Stars Fell into the Sky*. Houghton Mifflin, 1992.
Simon, S. *Stars*. Morrow Junior Books, 1986.
Trapani, I. *Twinkle, Twinkle Little Star*. Whispering Coyote Press, 1994.

Portals for Expansion:

Social Studies
• Students can locate and mark important observatories on a map and explain how their locations deal with the findings in the lab.

Language Arts
• After reading the book, *Twinkle, Twinkle Little Star* (Trapani), students can write modern versions of the nursery rhyme or other poems related to the night sky.

Art
• Students can use light to create pieces of art using Lite Brite® or making suncatchers by gluing pieces of cellophane on frames to hang in your classroom windows.

Why Do Stars Twinkle?

Students should arrange themselves in a way that one student can point a flashlight at the group.

Procedure:

1. While the room lights are turned on, look at the flashlight's beam from across your classroom. Describe how it looks.

2. Turn out the room lights and observe the light. Does it look different? Describe it.

3. Clap an eraser near the flashlight. How does the dust change the way the light looks?

4. Put a red filter or a piece of red cellophane on the flashlight. Does the red light look brighter or more dull than the light without cellophane?

   Is the red light brighter as it passes through chalk dust? _____

5. Put a blue filter or a piece of blue cellophane on the flashlight. Does the blue light look brighter or more dull than the light without cellophane?

   Is the blue light brighter as it passes through chalk dust? _____

6. Observe what happens when your teacher lights a candle and places it 10 cm in front of the flashlight. How bright is the beam of light as it passes through the heat coming from the candle?

Questions:

1. Why are astronomical observatories often found on hilltops?

2. Why are astronomical observatories often found in remote areas?

Launching Water Rockets

Purpose:
- Build a water bottle rocket constructed from a 2-liter plastic soda bottle.
- Launch the rocket using an air pump as an ignition device.
- Calculate the height of the launch based on mathematical principles.

Materials Needed:

Launch Device:
bicycle pump with
   air pressure gauge
rubber hose
rubber stopper
silicon seal (rubber bathroom sealant)
tire valve
ring stand
brick
books
copper tubing (short piece)

Sighting Device:
protractor and ruler
fishing line
nut and bolt, small washer

Bottle Rocket:
2-liter plastic soda bottle
6" (152 mm) piece of
   ¾" (19 mm) PVC pipe

Procedure: See student lab sheets for instructions.

Behind the Scenes: The water in the bottle serves as fuel and the rocket will launch when the fuel is forced out of the bottle by the build up of air pressure. It is a demonstration of Newton's Third Law explaining that for every action there is an equal and opposite reaction. By varying the amount of fuel and pressure, different action/reactions will occur and the rocket will travel to various heights. The same holds true for a space shuttle launch. The components such as the mass of the shuttle and pull of the earth's gravity all take part in determining how much fuel is needed to launch a shuttle into orbit.

Answer Key For Questions:
1. Answers will vary. For example, if too much water is loaded, then the height will not be as great.
2. Answers will vary. For example, enough fuel is needed to reach orbit, but not so much as to have any left over.
3. Answers will vary. For example, more pressure means higher altitude and too much or too little water means lower altitude.

Literature Links: Bendick, J. *Space Travel*. Franklin Watts, 1982.
Cole, J. *The Magic School Bus Lost in the Solar System*. Scholastic, 1990.
Rockwell, A., & Brown, D. *Space Vehicles*. Dutton Children's Books, 1994.

Portals for Expansion:

Math

- Have students predict how high their rockets will go before they actually launch them. Compare their predictions to the actual height of the rockets. Using the chart, interested students may determine the height of the launch based on the angle of the sighting device.

Science

- Research the history of space rockets. Find out how rockets are made and what propels them into space.

Language Arts

- Students can be "reporters" covering the rocket launch. Have them interview spectators and participants in the launch, and then write stories for the classroom newspaper or make an AV announcement describing the outcome of the rocket launch.
- Write a story about life on another planet, a space station, or on a spaceship. Illustrate the stories and include them in the classroom library.

Health

- Design a balanced meal for a day in space or a week on a space station. Have students determine what can be eaten in space due to packaging requirements.
- Contact the NASA web site to find out information on what foods the astronauts eat in space and how the foods are prepared. Interested in more information and cool space stuff? Contact the NASA Observatorium.

  Web sites:
  http://shuttle.nasa.gov/index.html/
  http://observe.ivv.nasa.gov/nasa/core.shtml

Art

- Construct a rocket launch site model for the classroom. Students can display their rockets in the launch site prior to the day of "blast off."

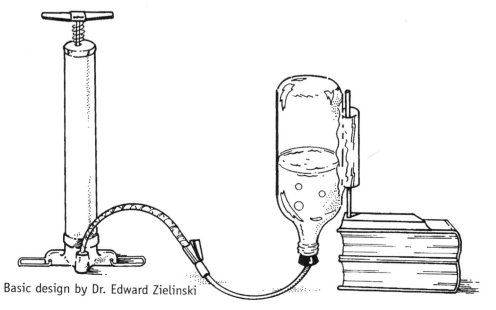

Basic design by Dr. Edward Zielinski

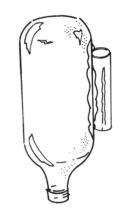

Launching Water Rockets

Rocket Construction:

1. Remove the label from a clean 2-liter bottle.
2. Take the piece of PVC pipe and attach it vertically to the side of the bottle with the silicone sealant. Make sure the pipe is straight on the bottle. A way to check is to roll the bottle along the table until the PVC pipe hits. Allow the sealant to dry over night.
3. Decorate the rocket using a variety of craft materials such as construction paper, glue, yarn, markers, etc.

Launch Device and Sighting Device:

1. Build the sighting device by following the diagram.

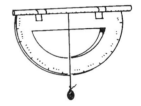

2. Build the launch device by following the diagram.

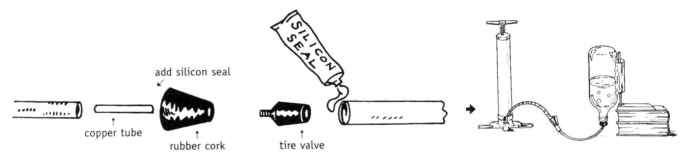

add silicon seal

copper tube

rubber cork

tire valve

Prepare the Launch Site: Choose a launch site. Mark off a spot that is 30.5 m from the launch site. This will be the point at which the Sighter (uses the sighting device) stands.

Launching The Rocket:

1. On the day of the launch, measure in milliliters the amount of water that is put into the rocket for fuel. *Note:* The amount of water in rockets should differ. No bottle should be completely full.
2. Place the rubber stopper of the launch device tightly into the mouth of the bottle.
3. Quickly invert the bottle and place the PVC pipe onto the rod of the launch stand.
4. Work in teams of three or more students. One student should hold the bottle in place by holding the mouth of the bottle and rubber stopper. **Safety Note:** Do not tightly grip the bottle and stopper but allow the rocket to launch when it begins to move.
5. Another student pumps the bicycle pump forcing air to flow into the bottle. Watch for bubbles coming up through the water as air is pumped into the bottle.
6. Once the bottle launches, determine the amount of air pressure that was exerted by reading the gauge. Fill in the chart. The Sighter provides the height of the launch.

LAB
Astronomy

Launching Water Rockets–Collecting Data

Procedure: 1. Measure the amount of water in milliliters that is placed in your rocket. Record your answer in the column "Volume of Water."

2. Launch your rocket. Once the bottle launches, determine the amount of air pressure that was exerted by reading the gauge and complete the pressure column on the chart.

3. Ask the Sighter what the reading was for your rocket at its apogee. *Note:* Use the number that is greater than 90° on the protractor. Record the angle in the column "Reading at Apogee."

4. Subtract 90° from your reading. Record your answer.

5. Determine the height of the launch by comparing your angle to the Chart for Launch Height which will indicate the height of the launch. Record the height.

6. Keep accurate records of the weight of each rocket, the amount of water used as fuel, and the pressure applied before releasing each rocket.

Rocket Launch Data Table

Launch Number	Pressure	Volume of Water	Reading at Apogee	Angle minus 90	Height of Launch

Questions: 1. Describe what happened to the rocket launch when you placed more water into the rocket compared to when you placed less water in the rocket.

2. Why is the amount of fuel important when the space shuttle is launched?

3. Describe the relationship between the pressure, amount of water, and the height of the launch.

Chart for Launch Height

Angle (in degrees)	Launch Height (in meters)	Angle (in degrees)	Launch Height (in meters)	Angle (in degrees)	Launch Height (in meters)
1	.53	31	18.30	61	55.02
2	1.07	32	19.06	62	57.37
3	1.60	33	19.83	63	59.87
4	2.14	34	20.59	64	62.53
5	2.67	35	21.35	65	65.42
6	3.20	36	32.17	66	68.50
7	3.75	37	23.00	67	71.86
8	4.27	38	23.82	68	75.49
9	4.82	39	24.71	69	79.45
10	5.37	40	25.62	70	83.81
11	5.95	41	26.54	71	88.57
12	6.48	42	27.48	72	93.88
13	7.02	43	28.46	73	99.77
14	7.63	44	29.46	74	106.35
15	8.17	45	30.50	75	113.83
16	8.75	46	31.60	76	122.34
17	9.30	47	32.70	77	132.13
18	9.91	48	33.86	78	143.50
19	10.49	49	35.08	79	156.92
20	11.10	50	36.36	80	172.97
21	11.71	51	37.67	81	192.58
22	12.32	52	39.04	82	217.01
23	12.96	53	40.47	83	248.39
24	13.57	54	41.97	84	290.18
25	14.21	55	43.55	85	348.62
26	14.88	56	45.23	86	436.18
27	15.52	57	46.97	87	581.97
28	16.23	58	48.80	88	873.40
29	16.90	59	50.75	89	1747.35
30	17.63	60	52.83	90	----